Layout and Printing: Keterpress Enterprises, Jerusalem

Translated by Alan Clayman

Photographs © Aliza Auerbach

pp. 6–7, At Yad Vashem, Jerusalem
pp. 8–9, The old Train Station, Jerusalem
Photos of the ocean from *The Song of the Sea*, Aliza Auerbach (2005–2007).

ISBN: 978-965-229-586-6

1 3 5 7 9 8 6 4 2

Gefen Publishing House Ltd.
6 Hatzvi Street
Jerusalem 94386, Israel
972-2-538-0247
orders@gefenpublishing.com

Gefen Books
11 Edison Place
Springfield, NJ 07081
516-593-1234
orders@gefenpublishing.com

www.gefenpublishing.com

Printed in Israel

Library of Congress Cataloging-in-Publication Data

Auerbach, Aliza.
[Nitsolim. English]
Survivors / Aliza Auerbach.
p. cm.
ISBN 978-965-229-586-6

1. Holocaust survivors-Israel-Portraits.   2. Holocaust, Jewish (1939-1945)—Personal narratives.
3. Older people-Israel-Portraits.   4. Photography, Artistic. I. Title.

CT1919.P345A8913 2012
940.53'180922-dc23
2012023870

SURVIVORS

ALIZA AUERBACH

gefen
publishing house
JERUSALEM ◆ NEW YORK Est. 1981

Preface

A short personal history: In 1933 my father, Georg-Gideon Auerbach, who was born in Cologne, Germany, read Hitler's book, *Mein Kampf*, and believed every word written there. He understood he had to leave Germany. He had just finished his PhD in chemistry but could not find a job. Since he was not a Zionist but held left-wing views, he decided to try his luck in Russia. He traveled there to prepare the ground for himself and his new bride, my mother, whom he had just married. However, there too – this time on account of his German citizenship – he remained unemployed. He returned to Germany, collected his wife and together they traveled to Turkey. My mother, who was already well advanced in pregnancy, felt out of place there. A Zionist friend who paid them a visit in Istanbul on his way to Palestine, and who saw the poor conditions in which my parents-to-be were living, had a word with them. "You will find conditions just as bad in Palestine," he promised, "but at least you'll be in your own country."

For the birth of their first daughter they returned to Germany. However, three months later, at the end of 1934, the small family arrived in Haifa and started to build a new life there. My father, who began his professional career as an unskilled worker at the Shemen factory, in time became the production manager at the Blueband Margarine factory. The family had three more daughters, and over time thirteen grandchildren and twenty-one great-grandchildren.

My father's repeated attempts to warn his parents and sister of the approaching danger all failed. My grandfather replied that Germany was a safe place and that nothing bad would happen to him there. My father's younger brother, Rudolf, who was an extreme idealist, preferred in 1936 to volunteer in the Spanish Civil War, where death found him. His burial place remains unknown to this day. My aunt managed to emigrate to America with her husband and was saved by the skin of her teeth. My grandparents fled Germany to Holland at the very last moment with just the clothes on their backs. From there they moved to England, where they just about managed to make a living. My grandmother, who had spent her entire life in a very large, affluent house surrounded by many servants, was employed as a day worker in a lace factory in Nottingham. Only later on did they join their daughter in America.

Just very recently I discovered, to my great astonishment, that my grandfather, my father's father, had been imprisoned in Dachau following Kristallnacht. Somehow, in a manner unknown to me, after seven months he was released. He lost thirty kilograms (sixty-five pounds) in the camp and never returned to his old self again. That is what my grandmother has recounted. It is inconceivable to me that even after this horrible experience, he still refused to see the writing on the wall.

I have been asked more than once what led me to work on such a difficult and complex subject as the Holocaust. After all, I am not what is known in Israel as a first-generation survivor, or even a second- or third-generation survivor. I would say there is not one answer. As so often happens, the answer lies in a sequence of events that took place over many years. Without my being aware of it at the time, they became formative events.

The Eichmann trial started in 1961, during my first year at the Hebrew University in Jerusalem. It took place at the Bet Ha'Am Community Center in Jerusalem (today the Gerard Bechar Center), not far from the small student room I was renting. I must confess it never occurred to me to go to the hall and listen to the testimonies. Only distant echoes of what was happening inside reached me.

One day, while I was walking with my then boyfriend, hugging, next to the Bet Ha'Am, a man suddenly stopped in front of us and shouted, "Aren't you ashamed? There they are talking about atrocities that even the devil himself could not invent, and you are going along as though it is business as usual..." I remember the sense of shame and discomfort to this very day.

I met my girlfriend R. a short while afterwards. This was for me a first direct encounter with someone who returned "from there." She was twelve years older than me, from Poland, the only one left from her entire family. I saw the deep scar on her thigh for the first time when we went together to the swimming pool. She told me then that she had been injured when, at the age of fourteen, she jumped from the train that was taking her to one of those hellholes whose name she did not even know. The cattle wagon on the way to hell, in which she traveled, was already full of countless bodies, onto which she and her friend on the voyage clambered, in order to wriggle through the barbed wire that blocked the little window. Together they managed to part the barbed wire, to make an opening that would let a body through. Their hands were bleeding but they felt nothing. The main thing was to get out, to breathe some air.

Her friend, who was her senior, jumped first. Immediately after the jump a shot was heard. R. understood what had happened, yet still jumped after her. She lowered herself down, sticking closely to the wall of the wagon. Death was not frightening. Life with all its tortures was. For some reason, they didn't shoot at her. Maybe the soldiers on the roof didn't notice her. From the intensity of the fall onto a rock or sharp stone, copious blood flowed from her thigh; it wouldn't stop until she put some leaves on it that she found in the field.

Thus began a long voyage in time. We would meet almost every evening in my room, and she would just keep telling more and more stories, into the small hours of the night. Up to then she had been unable to talk to anyone about that period, she said.

Years later I had a boyfriend who had also survived the Shoah. He was fourteen years old when his mother was murdered before his eyes by a Nazi commander and he saw life dwindling away slowly from his father through hunger and typhoid in the camp. His entire family was exterminated. This was my second intimate meeting with the Other Planet. He too shared with me what happened to him in those terrible times.

There are certain things that sink into one's soul and float to the surface all of a sudden, as though they had waited all that time for just the right moment, to return, to rise up and to be present.

And so, one day, over eight years ago, while I was watching one of the documentaries on Holocaust Memorial Day, I suddenly knew that the survivors with their families would be the subject of my next book. This work, the third volume of a trilogy, will complete the two books *Rishonim* (Pioneers, 1990) and *Olim* (New Immigrants, 1992; English edition entitled *Aliyah*).

I wanted to create a photo album that would show the survivors as they are today, with the emphasis on hope, on the miracle of rehabilitation, the power of survival, on the unbelievable wonder of continuity, in spite of everything. The human brain is not built to hold and absorb the dimensions of this enormous horror, and it transforms the unacceptable number of six million Jews exterminated into some sort of anonymous information. I thought that the personal stories of several survivors – isolated bits of life and hope in a huge, raging sea of death and loss – would somehow illustrate the enormous loss and transform the inconceivable numbers into people of flesh and blood.

For many years, actually all through my work, I have dealt in one way or another with the cycle of life: with the beginning which is an end, and with the end which is always also a new beginning. This cycle of life into which we entered – perhaps without our consent – never ceases to puzzle me and make me wonder.

I understood that the encounter with the survivors and their stories would not be easy. So I decided at the same time to photograph the sea, a subject that I had always wanted to deal with but had never dared. I thought the sea would soothe me. And so it was indeed at the beginning. As I advanced, the sea drew me to it for nearly two years, and left no room to photograph the survivors. I was probably too scared to be drawn into the hell of the Holocaust and preferred to immerse myself in the comforting depths of the sea. That is how it came about that I started my work on this book over eight years ago, but stopped photographing for a period, during which time things crystallized and ripened within me.

I had to come to several decisions about dealing with the subject: I thought it was right to photograph survivors who were representative of as many as possible of the communities that suffered during World War II. This is why I went looking for survivors from Bulgaria, Libya and Tunis, alongside those from Poland, Germany and Holland. Some of them felt uncomfortable being called "survivors," because they were just exiled to labor camps, or forced to leave their homes for a limited period of time, and did not experience the Shoah in all its cruelty like the rest of Europe's Jews.

I also decided, after much hesitation, to concentrate on survivors who built their homes in Israel. In no way do I criticize those who chose to build their lives in their countries of origin or in other countries; it was rather a natural continuation to my two books mentioned earlier, *Rishonim* (Pioneers) and *Olim/*

Aliyah (New Immigrants), which one way or another focused on the experience of immigration to Israel.

I understood from the very beginning that it was not for me to set criteria for suffering. There were those who survived the extermination camps after their families were murdered in front of their eyes, and those who literally already had the hangman's noose around their necks, and yet they still managed, it would appear, to return to an everyday life, with joy, fully functioning. And there are those who had "only" lost their homes or been sent to labor camps, yet their worlds had been shattered. Nightmares haunt their nights until today, and they pass their days like leaves blowing in the wind. Who can understand the complexity and diversity of the human soul?

So I photographed those who had survived the fiery furnace alongside those who fled their homes and hid. All of them are survivors.

I asked every survivor to write a short text about his or her life. Here and there I wrote down what the survivor said, but only when he made it clear he could not handle it himself. I only edited the texts slightly, in order to keep the personal, individual style. Therefore I did not, as it is called in editing, try to "standardize" the texts. I hoped that way the reader would get a feel for the character of the person, not just through the photograph but also through the way he expressed himself and the details he chose to recount. And perhaps beyond that – through his silence, the words he did not say.

Some of the survivors preferred to speak about themselves in the third person, since still today they are incapable of identifying the adult they have become with the child or young person who went through the valley of the shadow of death. For others, their mechanisms of repression and denial totally erased the horrors, so that today they only remember a fraction and to most of the questions posed, they answered, "I don't remember," "Perhaps," "A long time has gone by," and similar responses. There were also those who were pleased to be photographed and agreed to tell their stories – but only to me, and not until I promised that what they said would not be written or come out in any other way. So I found myself the keeper of stories that had not yet been told, even to their closest family.

And yet I believe that these stories, each one recounted in its own way and style, paint a picture of

the darkest period in modern times, perhaps even in history, in which, as one of the survivors wrote, "The human lexicon has still not invented the words that can describe it."

I did not want to include in the book family photographs of dear ones who had been murdered, but rather to photograph objects that remained: from the Shoah period itself, and also from the preceding period, as a testimony to a home that existed and is no more.

It is amazing what power is concealed within an object, the multitude of memories that emerge from it and how terrible are the pictures folded up inside one small, innocent-looking little object.

For example, take the lemon of Ruti Ma'ayan (see p. 174). An entire life story is wrapped up in this brown lemon, hard as stone, shriveled and shrunken, that nevertheless kept its original form. Only sixty years have passed, yet it looks like something found during an archaeological dig from the First Temple period. As though the hell of those days has passed it through thousands of years, using a time machine. The lemon was thrown at the train in which Ruti and her family were sent to the camp in 1943, by the nurses working in the Jewish Hospital in Czernovitz. They knew what the overcrowding was like in the wagons and presumably hoped the smell of the fresh lemon would help bring some relief. Ruti caught the lemon and kept it with her throughout the exhausting journey. When they reached the camp Ruti's mother hid it in a small niche in the wall of the hut where they lived. Every few days Ruti would check if the lemon was still there. At some point her mother wanted to throw away the dried-up, useless fruit, but Ruti announced that she would be liberated with the lemon. So from its place in the wall, the lemon experienced what happened to Ruti... Afterwards it was with her when she came to Israel, at her wedding and the birth of her three children and seven grandchildren, a constant reminder of the hell that had been and a testimony to the conquering spirit of life.

But the story doesn't end there. Years later, during a chance visit to an exhibition of paintings by the late Israeli artist Meir Pichhadze, Ruti suddenly saw a painting on canvas of a girl with two braids holding her lemon. How could it be? How did he know? Ruti fainted on the spot. Apparently, the full horror of that time came back to her when she saw the painting. On her way home by bus, her handbag – with the lemon that always accompanied her as an amulet inside it – was stolen. Ruti would not rest or give up. She put advertisements in the newspapers and addressed the anonymous thief in an emotional radio broadcast, in which she recounted the meaning of the lemon for her. And wonder of wonders – the lemon was returned to her. Today the lemon lies in a small wooden box, on a light-blue woolen mat, knitted by a friend's mother who did not survive the Shoah. The friend asked for these two objects to dwell together in the same little wooden box.

The story of a lemon. An ordinary, meaningless object to the innocent eye.

I have often wondered, why do survivors keep things that retain such difficult echoes of those dark times instead of destroying them? One of the survivors, Sarah Rubin, told me that she always hoped that one day those objects would serve as silent witnesses in the Big Trial that would be held. She also said that on sleepless nights, which were many, she would get up in the dead of night, take out from the drawer the yellow star and the numbers that had been sewn on her clothes and in front of a picture of her grandchildren and great-grandchildren would crumple up the bits of cloth in rage and mumble, "That is my answer to you, may your name be blotted out" (see p. 16).

I decided to photograph railway lines as a motif throughout the book. The railway lines long ago became an icon symbolizing the Shoah. I opted to take photographs right here, in Jerusalem. I photographed them on one bitter-cold winter day, when they suddenly looked like they were "there." I wanted to emphasize by doing so that we carry with us this seal wherever we go.

I chose to photograph the families as though I were a family member photographing my family. I didn't want staged, cold, alien studio portraits. I wanted to give the direct warm feeling of an unprofessional photo. So I made do with the natural conditions I found, with no special lighting. These photos in general raised problems I had not expected at the start. The little ones in the group didn't always have the required patience for a group photo. This is why one can sometimes find them photographed with their eyes closed or with some of their faces obscured. Moreover, to get dozens of people together at a given time, on a given day and at a given place was no simple task. Some-

times someone was missing and I didn't manage to photograph the entire family, but I thought that even if some family member were missing, those present would be sufficient to testify to the wonderful miracle of the continuation of the line.

Many of the survivors thought, and still think, that bringing up a marvelous family was the ultimate answer to the attempted annihilation by that demon known as Hitler. The "answers" are many and varied: families of just two children and two grandchildren, next to families with dozens of children, grandchildren and great-grandchildren. Ultra-Orthodox families and secular families, traditional families and those living on kibbutzim, and not a few mixed families, where the religious, secular and ultra-Orthodox live side by side, all children of the same parents!

I had the honor to photograph Shulamit Catane, an eighty-seven-year-old survivor from France, holding on her lap Hallel, then her latest, the 140th great-grandchild, the day after she was born. Shulamit is blessed with ten children and eighty-one grandchildren. Some weeks ago I called Shulamit up to find out how she was doing. She was as clear and joyous as ever and was boasting that she now has 205 great-grandchildren, with six more on the way (that she knows of) – and she remembers the names of all of them! Every evening before going to sleep she blesses each and every one of them in her heart. What a magnificent "answer"! What a vast range of families, but a single, winning answer – the power of life – its limits and borders who can fathom?

Three years have passed since the Hebrew edition of this volume was published, and I am happy to present this new edition for the English-speaking public. I would like to dedicate this English volume, as well, to the survivors, wherever they are, and in this way to express my admiration and appreciation – for their courage, determination, will power and strength. This book is yet another testimony to the power of the human spirit.

Aliza Auerbach, Jerusalem, June 2012

Sarah Rubin – Poland

I was born in 1928 to the late Malka and Moshe Brodbecker. I grew up in a happy, wealthy home, well organized in every sense. As recounted within the family, I was a good and easy child, with lots of friends.

From the age of six I attended three schools: (1) a general Polish school – mandatory education; (2) Bet Yaacov, because we were *charedim*, ultra-Orthodox Jews, where we studied Judaism, education, Jewish history and Jewish law; and (3) Bet HaTarbut, the "House of Culture," where I studied Zionist history and tales of Jewish courage. I am grateful to all three, but the best education of all I received at home, from the family. My late mother was a major educational personality at that time.

To my regret, all this goodness ended too early.

In 1939 the Second World War broke out. Life changed in one fell swoop. Those human animals that are called the Germans put a stop to normal life.

In 1940, we were moved to the Strachowice ghetto, which was closed shortly thereafter, and the number of inmates declined. In February 1940, at the age of twelve, I found myself working twelve hours a day at the Hermann Goering (may his name be blotted out) arms factory. I suffered from hunger, cold and sadness for my large family, which had been reduced to such a miserable life. I suffered beatings and every sort of degradation that even paper cannot bear to hear about.

On October 10, 1942, there was an *Aktion*, a roundup. The entire family apart from my sister was expelled to Treblinka and there exterminated. I was left an orphan in the world. I was not expelled, because I had a work permit, and I continued to work at the labor camp.

At the end of 1943 I came with the whole group to Auschwitz. Here began the hell that human animals had created. The human lexicon has still not invented the words that can define it. I experienced several Selections by Mengele, may his name be blotted out. Despite typhoid and all the other problems, faith and hope never left me, thanks to the excellent education I had received and the prayers I muttered all the time.

On December 24, 1944, we were transferred as a group of five hundred women to a labor camp in Germany, which was no better than Auschwitz.

In February 1945 I was moved to the Theresienstadt death camp.

In March 1945 I took three potatoes I had found in the field and was sentenced to hanging. When the noose was around my neck, the Allies bombed the camp and I was saved. A large scar on my neck remains with me to this day.

Thank God, on May 8, 1945, came the liberation. For me it was an enormous disappointment. I had imagined everything would go back to the way it had been, but I found myself alone in a cruel world. I summoned all my emotional and physical strength with great hope for the future. The will to live is very strong.

From 1945 to 1946 I stayed with a group of children at an orphanage in Prague. In 1946 I moved to a kibbutz in Greifenberg, Germany. At the beginning of 1947 I moved to France, and there, in Lechutet, near Marseille, we waited for the arrival of a boat to take us to Palestine.

In 1947 I made aliyah on board the *Latrun*, but was returned together with my sister to Cyprus, where we stayed about half a year.

In 1947, in Palestine, a new and difficult chapter in my life began. That was a daily war for survival. I studied and worked. I had spent the entire war together with my sister, may she have a long life, and in Israel we helped each other as much as possible.

In 1950 I married and, thank God, was blessed to raise a family. I had three children, as they say in Yiddish, *tzu Gott un tzu leit* ["to God and to people" – good and beloved both by God and by people]. All my children studied, and all have degrees and also studied in yeshivot, because it was forbidden for me to forget from where I had come. My husband, who should have a long life, and I achieved everything through hard work and savings, and we have always been happy with our lot. Does it not say, "Who is rich? He who is happy with his lot"?

I am blessed, thank God, with nineteen grandchildren and great-grandchildren, and I always make the *Shehecheyanu* blessing [the benediction for happy occasions]. Because this is my consolation and my revenge against human evil. Peace and love, understanding, faith, reliability and friendship, thank God, reign in my family. There are no secrets between us and no disagreements. All for one and one for all.

However, I still miss my late mother. I cannot forget her wisdom, modesty, honesty, love and warmth that she radiated to one and all. I very much want to be like her, but I haven't been so successful.

I have written briefly about a life of almost seventy years, which has included joy, suffering, sadness and renewal to a new life, and again joy and the creation, achievements, building and continuation of the generations for ever more.

Sarah Rubin, Bnei Brak

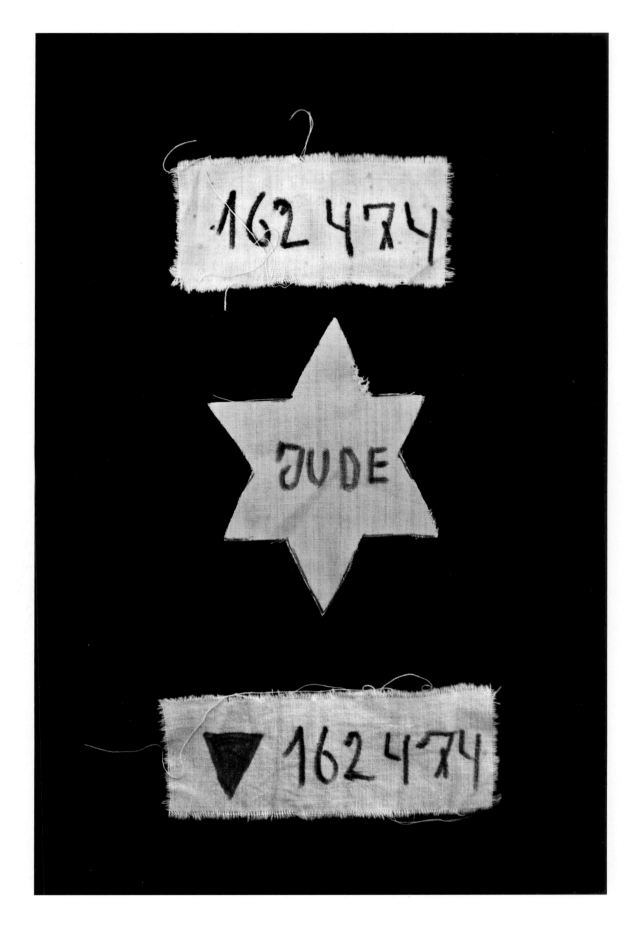

Serial numbers and star that were sewn onto a garment at the Strachowice camp. Redrawn by Sarah Rubin because they had faded in the wash.

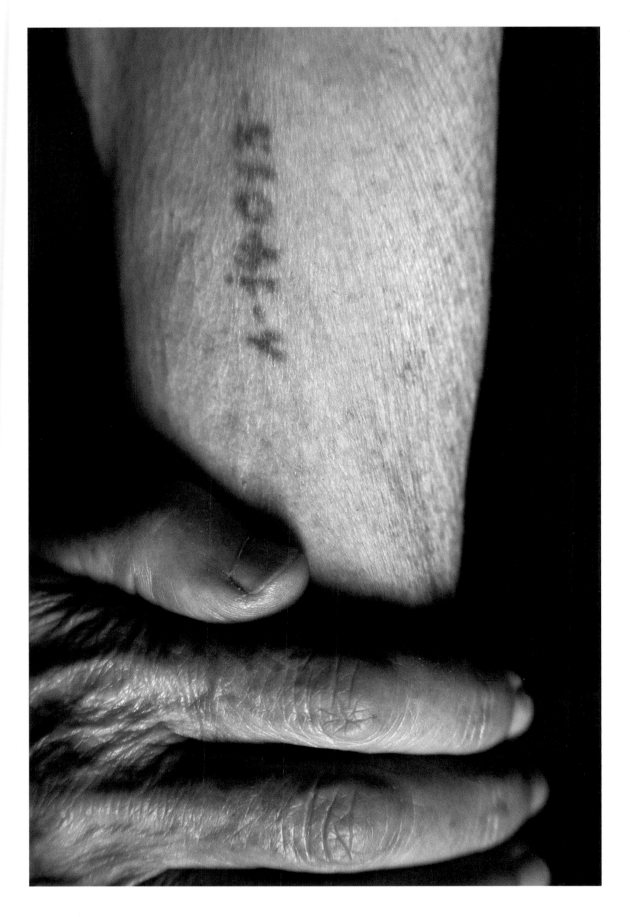

[pp. 18–19] Armband worn on the sleeve in the Strachowice ghetto. This was also redrawn by Sarah Rubin because it had been washed and become faded.

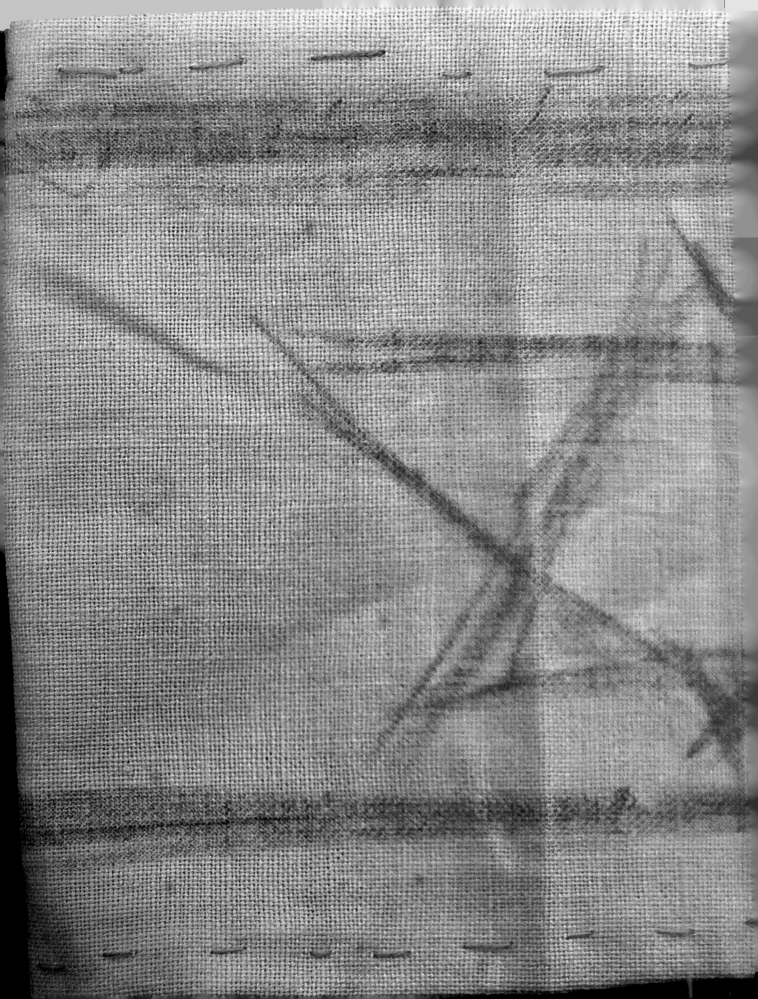

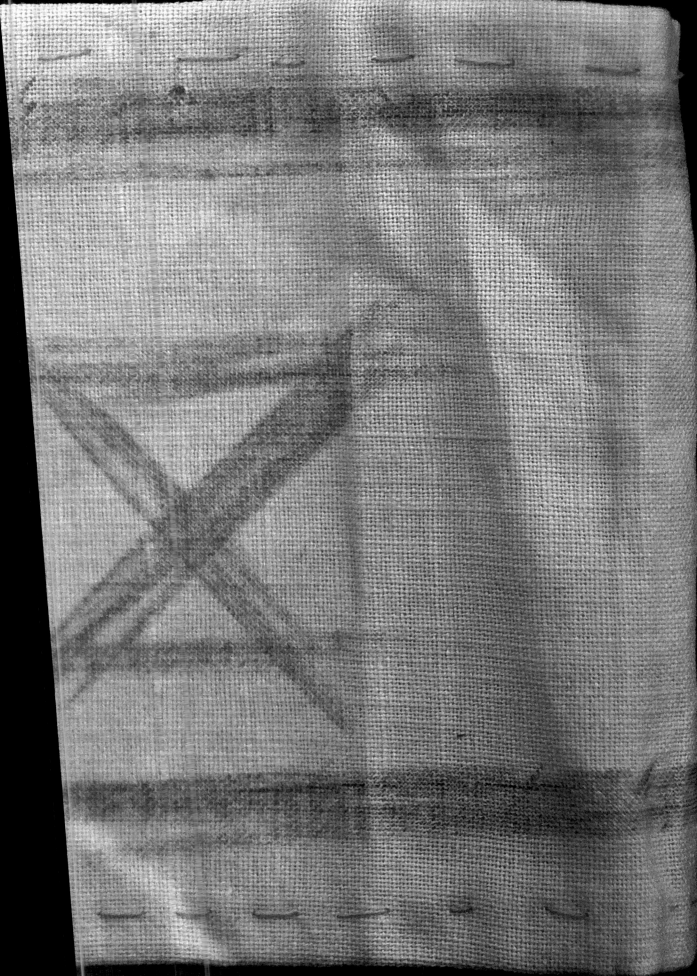

Yehuda Rubin – Poland

I was born in Lodz in 1924 to Chava née Gottgold and Yechiel. My father was a shoe sole cutter and my mother, like most of the women at that time, was a housewife. My grandmother and aunt lived in our house too. Our home was a religious one and I learned in a *cheder* [religious elementary school]. I recall that we celebrated my bar mitzvah with the family still outside the ghetto.

In 1940 they transferred us to the Lodz ghetto. We took with us whatever could be taken from the home. We broke all the furniture of the house so that we could heat the small room where we lived in the ghetto. At the beginning in the ghetto I worked with my father. Later I changed jobs and worked rolling cigarettes.

Most of the family had already been sent to Chelmno in 1940, where they were killed. My mother and younger brother, Avram, were caught in one of the roundups in 1941 and also sent to Chelmno. They too were murdered there. In 1944 I was separated from my father. They sent me to the Czestochowa camp. My father was sent to another camp, in Germany. In Czestochowa I worked in an arms factory, Varta. The conditions in the camp were terrible. I was on my feet all day at a machine that put lead into bullets. I had to meet an enormous quota, and if I failed, I was savagely beaten.

In January 1945, I was liberated when the Russians arrived and captured the camp. It was a particularly severe winter. I remember going out of the camp in the morning to look for bread. We saw a long line outside a bakery and joined it. Polish gentiles standing in the line said, "What, so many of you survived?"

Two weeks later, the survivors returned to Lodz. We hoped to find our relatives. We threw out a German who had moved into one of the houses of the Jews during the war, and we lived there. We stayed in Lodz until July 1945. We registered to go to Palestine and left Poland on our way to the Land of Israel. When we reached Italy we joined a kibbutz in a little town called Coli. There were about ninety of us, all survivors, mostly Hungarians. We boarded a ship called *Four Freedoms*. When we approached Haifa we were caught by the British and transferred to Cyprus. We were held there for six months, where we lived in tents and passed a very hard winter.

I knew that my aunt, my mother's sister, had already moved to Palestine in 1924. I remembered her name but not the exact address. Nonetheless I wrote her a letter, which miraculously she received. That's how our correspondence started, and in the end I received a permit to return to Israel. This time I arrived on a regular ship. A friend was waiting for me and took me to my aunt's home. At first I worked at all sorts of odd jobs, until eventually I was given a job at the post office, where I worked for almost forty years, until I retired.

I learned of my father's fate from my uncle, who was with him in a labor camp in Germany. He died a month before the liberation.

I met my wife, Sarah, in 1949, and we married in 1950.

We have three children and today we are blessed with a large number of grandchildren and great-grandchildren. Three months ago a new great-granddaughter was born.

Yehuda Rubin, Bnei Brak

Money from the Lodz ghetto

Sarah and Yehuda Rubin in their home in Bnei Brak

The Rubin family at a *sheva berachot* celebration in Bnei Brak, following the wedding of their grandson

Zev Birger – Lithuania

I was born in the city of Kovno, Lithuania, in 1926, to my parents, Feige Zippora née Kaplan and my father, Pinchas Birger. There was a great deal of harmony in our home. My parents had firm Zionist beliefs and a strong faith in the need to create a Jewish national home in the Land of Israel. Yet they kept a traditional lifestyle. We observed the Sabbath, we went to synagogue on the High Holy Days, and were particular to eat kosher.

My mother had a very delicate temperament. She was wise and talented, and radiated warmth and unique kind-heartedness. We were greatly influenced by her character. Just one small example: her older sister, who was married and a mother to two little girls, had been murdered by the Bolsheviks in 1917. My mother, who was then still an unmarried girl, traveled to her sister's home and took the two orphaned girls. To her own wedding she brought two ready-made daughters...

The outbreak of the World War at the beginning only affected Lithuania marginally. However, in September 1940, Lithuania was annexed to the Soviet Union. I can still hear the noise of the tanks rolling down the street. That very day Zionist organizations were banned. Many, including my parents, thought that Soviets were preferable to Germans, but the confiscation of property and the persecution of the Lithuanian middle class, among whom were many Jews, started immediately.

In the middle of June 1941, the German attack on the Soviet Union started, and within a week the whole of Lithuania was in their hands. Lithuanian hooligans did whatever they wanted, plundered and murdered Jews indiscriminately. In July they started to gather all the Jews in the Slobodka ghetto, a suburb of Kovno. We left behind almost all our property and went to live in one small room in the ghetto. Every so often there was a roundup where they would randomly select groups of Jews and take them to be killed, either on the spot or at the Ninth Fort.

I can never forget the roundup of children on March 27, 1944, which lasted two days. The Germans insisted on taking all the children and went from house to house to drag them from their hiding places. The cries and desperate screams of the bereaved mothers still ring in my ears today. I can also still hear today the silence that enveloped the ghetto afterwards, without the shouts and laughter of children.

Already at the beginning of the war I had been one of the founders of the Bnei Zion (Children of Zion) Organization, which provided Zionist education to Jewish youth. We also brought out a magazine, *The Spark*, which was published during the resistance years in Lithuania, in the ghetto and even in the camp, where five editions in the handwriting of its editor, Shlomo Frankel, came out until the liberation. Our activity continued in the ghetto; among other things, we built bunkers at night where we stored food and water so that we could survive in them for a time.

Every so often I would take off the yellow star, put on a peaked cap and go out of the ghetto. That's how I would get food for my family. That's how I saw the Lithuanians and Ukrainians, who were devotedly serving in the SS, taking perverse pleasure from the distress of the Jews, who were marched all together to the workplaces to which they were attached.

On July 8, 1944, it was decided to clear the ghetto of all its inhabitants. On July 13, after we had succeeded in hiding in a bunker for five days, the Germans found us. They marched us with the handful left in the ghetto, about three hundred people, toward the railway station. On the way they separated out the men, and my mother was sent with the elderly and the sick to the left. That was the last time I saw her. The sight of her, holding her hands in prayer, won't leave me at night until today. They loaded us onto freight trains in the direction of Germany. My brother and I could have jumped from the train on several occasions, but we didn't want to part from our father.

We reached the Stutthoff camp, and from there a few days later we got to Dachau. Several days later we were moved to Kaufring No. 4 camp, where we did forced labor in the Germans' armaments industry, in an underground factory manufacturing planes. When I had to carry a thirty-kilogram [sixty-five-pound] block of wood through heavy snow, shod in paper shoes made from cement sacks, and heavy wooden clogs tied with steel wire to my legs, I would repeat to myself over and over, like I used to convince myself every morning and evening, "Valik, you can. It's not heavy. Walk. Walk. Forward. Forward. You'll get out alive."

When my father died in my arms in the camp from a bad infection, and when my brother was sent to another work camp, I was left alone. "What's the point of all this?" I thought to myself when I was transferred to Camp 5 and Camp 7, which were even worse. Yet, right away the refrain came back to peck away and not leave me alone. "You will survive. That will be our revenge."

On April 27, 1945, the liberation came in the form of American soldiers driving jeeps. An American officer transferred me to the hospital at Bad Wörishofen even though they had already despaired of saving my life, but they succeeded in healing my body, which was full of abscesses. I

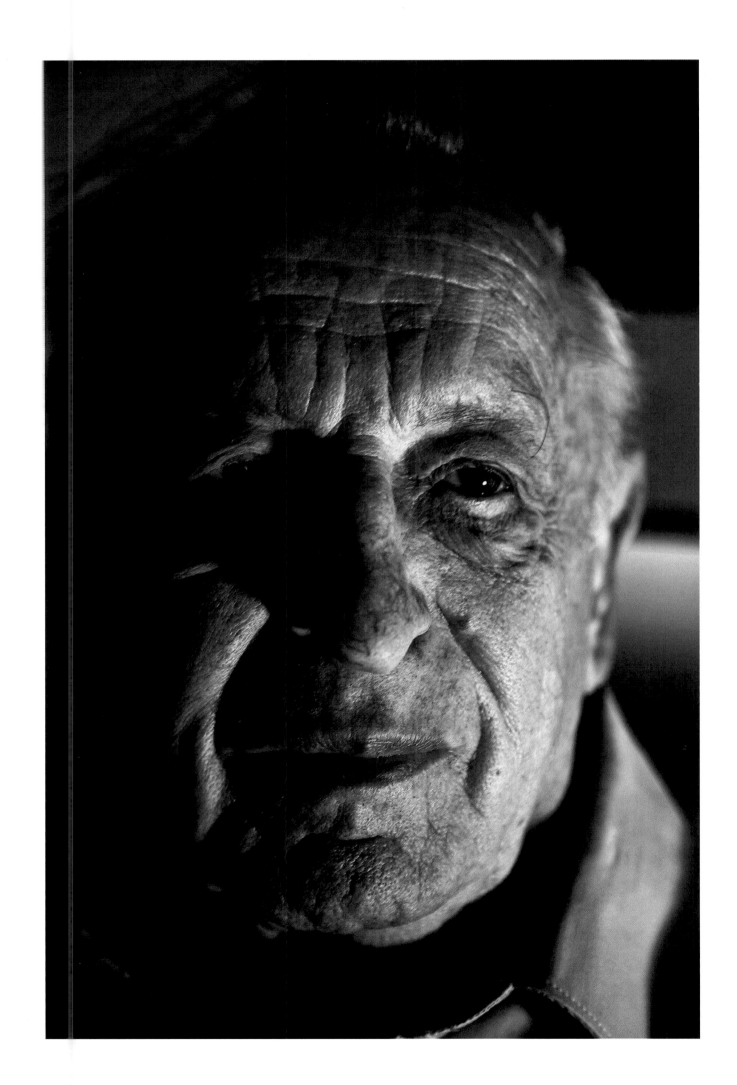

was attached by the American officer to their unit as an interpreter, I received a US Army uniform and I became one of them. Even though the commander kept pleading with me to return with his troops to the USA and get US citizenship, I convinced him that my place was in Israel, because we had to build a state for the Jewish people, so that something like this would never happen again. We parted with a heavy heart.

I traveled to Frankfurt, and as part of Aliyah Bet I was involved in moving Holocaust survivors to Palestine. There I met my future wife. In July 1946, I married Trudy Simon, and on November 20, 1947, I disembarked at Haifa with my new family, my beloved wife and mother-in-law.

When the War of Independence broke out, I enlisted in the army. After I was released from military service, we settled in Haifa and I worked in the port in the Customs and Excise Department. When the customs offices were moved to Jerusalem, a task I was assigned to carry out, we also moved to live in the capital. At that time I continued my studies at the Hebrew University in Jerusalem.

As part of my work at the Ministry of Trade and Industry, I worked a great deal on promoting the movies sector (the Israel Movies Center), publishing and design and generally advancing industry in Israel. After I retired from public service, I managed the company ICN in Europe. In 1982 I was asked by Teddy Kollek, then mayor of Jerusalem, to help in return for a salary of just one shekel per year to develop industry and tourism in the city. So I took on the position of manager of the Jerusalem International Book Fair, which I still do to this day. The Jerusalem Book Fair has become one of the most important book fairs in the world, at which well-known publishers from dozens of countries around the world attend.

In 2000 I received the Yakir Yerushalayim (Distinguished Citizen of Jerusalem) award in recognition of my efforts over many years to promote culture, business and tourism in Jerusalem. In 2001 I published my memoirs under the title *No Time for Patience*, which has been translated into several languages and published in six countries.

Trudy and I have had three sons, Doron, Oded and Gil, and over the years we have been blessed with eleven grandchildren. I consider myself lucky. I am so pleased that our children and their families maintain the values of Trudy and her family and those of my parents. Words such as love, warmth, friendship, responsibility, tolerance and volunteering are not empty words in their families. They

are filled with responsibility and love in their roles as educators, and in carrying out their duty to their country. In my opinion, that's the right answer to the Shoah: we cannot undo what was done, but we can prevent its repetition – in every possible way.

Zev Birger, Jerusalem

Zev Birger and his three sons

The Birger family in Jerusalem. In the background is a portrait of the late Trudy Birger, a survivor from Germany and Zev's wife.

All railway images were photographed in Jerusalem in the winter of 2008.

Laura Saporta-Stroumsa — Greece

I was born in Athens in 1925, the only daughter of Frieda Kimchi-Saporta and Jacques Saporta. I was eighteen when one night the Germans came to the house. My father made it clear we were Spanish and that the Spanish consulate had extended its protection to its Jewish citizens and guaranteed that they had nothing to fear. However, the next day, they called all the Spanish families from the consulate, informing us we had to gather at the synagogue to travel to Spain.

So in 1944 we came together with another forty-five families in the synagogue. Consular employees accompanied us to the railway with flowers. We boarded a very nice, regular train. After about 200 km the train stopped in the middle of a field, and suddenly Germans who had been waiting there appeared. They took us off the train, beat us and loaded us into a cattle train. We all stood in the middle of the wagon. They put out a container of water and something to eat, and then the train started to move off. On the train there was just one single small window. Everyone asked where we were going but we got no answer. One man climbed up to the window to look out and saw we were in Germany.

In rows of five we walked a long time, until we saw in the distance a closed camp, which was Auschwitz. Everybody screamed. We entered huts. We were together the entire day. We didn't work. The Spaniards didn't work but were kept under starvation conditions. A few months later my mother became sick with dysentery. There were no medicines and the doctor sent her to the infirmary. There she got better food and recovered. But when she left, she became sick again. This happened three times.

My father had hidden dollars in the soles of his shoes. He wanted to see Mother. But she died that night. A few months later I came down with typhoid. My friends hid me in the coal shed.

In May 1945 we were liberated. The British took us to a small village of SS men that was completely empty, and we went to live in their houses. The British took me by plane with the sick to a hospital in Liege, Belgium. After a month I returned to life. I asked where my father was. It turned out he was in the same hospital but on a different floor.

Two nurses brought me to visit him. The doctors were unable to help him, and advised me to take him to Lyon. We reached Marseille. We were meant to get from there by boat to Greece. One friend recommended that we stay in Marseille. Everyone traveled to Greece, but I stayed to care for my father, who was suffering from cancer.

A cousin of my mother found me in Marseille and looked after me for three months. Meanwhile I had already met Jacques. I returned to Greece. In the meantime my father passed away and I informed Jacques by telegram. He invited me to visit him in Paris. After the mourning period I went to Paris dressed in black. I returned to Greece and corresponded with Jacques for a year. We decided to get married.

I returned to Paris, and in 1947 we married. Jacques both worked and studied, and within a year our first son was born. In all we had three children, a son and two daughters. In 1968 we moved to Israel in the footsteps of our eldest son.

Laura Stroumsa, Jerusalem

Jacques Stroumsa – Greece

I was born in Salonika in 1913. My father was Avraham, a teacher of Hebrew and Jewish studies at the Jewish community's Alsheikh School, while my mother, Dodon née Yoel, was a highly skilled seamstress. In Salonika, which was known as the Jerusalem of the Balkans, everyone spoke Ladino. I was the oldest of four children. Only my little sister remained alive. About two years before my bar mitzvah I started music lessons. The first year was with the mandolin, and after that on the violin. The music lessons were particularly important to me, and I was never prepared to miss them, even once.

I started my higher education studies in engineering in Marseille in 1930, much influenced by my math teacher, Engineer Leitmer. After a year I transferred to Paris to continue my studies. After graduating in electrical engineering in Paris in 1935, I traveled to Bordeaux. There I did another year in electrical engineering and at the conservatory. At the end of my studies I kept my promise to my father and returned alone to Salonika. My father had made me promise, before I left to study, to marry a girl from Salonika. On my return I was called up to the Greek army, and in the evenings I studied German, which later on helped me to stay alive. When Mussolini attacked Greece in October 1940, the Jewish youth, myself included, were sent to the front. Upon my return I married Nora, a Jewish girl from a distinguished family, whom I had known before.

The Germans held Salonika for three and a half years, until October 1944. On July 11, 1942, all the Jewish men in Salonika were called to Freedom Square where we underwent humiliations and beatings. That was how the annihilation of Salonika Jewry started.

On May 8, 1943, my family and I arrived at Birkenau by train from Salonika. There were 2,500 people on the train, of whom 1,685 were gassed to death that same day. A friend, a doctor from Salonika, managed to let me know what was happening in the camp. That day, when I understood that my wife, who had been eight months pregnant, my father and mother and my two brothers had all gone up in smoke just hours after our arrival, I almost went out of my mind.

After they had tattooed the number on my arm, they sent me to a hut where there were three-tier bunks. We were six hundred men in the hut. The hut commander was a German criminal. Yet, amazingly, the first evening he gathered us all together and asked who played an instrument. I could not think of playing music after what I had learned had happened to my family. But the prisoners in the hut pushed me to play. In the end I decided to play Mozart's violin concerto, without a score. All the prisoners in the hut were weeping. The hut commander came up to me and said "I'm a pianist. I'll make sure you play in the orchestra." That's how I came to be in the Birkenau orchestra, where I was appointed first violin.

For a month I played the violin at Birkenau. After exactly a month I was transferred with other professional prisoners from Birkenau to Auschwitz. We reached Auschwitz after a five-kilometer [three-mile] march, worn out and miserable. There I managed to escape hard labor and got professional work, after I explained to those in charge that I was an engineer. The commander of the office coddled me, and so saved my life. For me he was a saint. For a year and a half I wore civilian clothes all the time, and he helped me to get my sister and others to work in the factory. I stayed in this engineer's office until January 1945, when I was sent together with other prisoners from Auschwitz to Mauthausen. We got to the railway station where they loaded us into open wagons full of snow. There I also lost my best friend. In the morning we reached Mauthausen. After being transferred to other camps, we finally reached the Gusen 2 camp.

The Americans who arrived to liberate us on May 8, 1945, at seven in the evening, found a group of living skeletons. They threw us cigarettes – Lucky Strike. How ironic. The moment of liberation will remain etched on my memory forever. The next day we dragged ourselves with our last strength to the nearby town of Wals, where we entered the first hospital we saw. I was sick with typhus and was at death's door.

When I recovered, I asked to go to France, because going back to Greece was impossible. That's how I found myself in Paris. I decided to return to study at the College of Electricity. In Paris in 1947 I married Laura, who was also a survivor from Greece. We had a son and two daughters.

In 1968 we made aliyah to Israel because of our eldest, Guy, who decided to make aliyah in 1966, even before he was eighteen. I worked in the lighting department of the Electricity Company in the Jerusalem municipality. Only after I retired did I do my doctorate, at the Technion in Haifa.

I have six grandchildren and two great-grandchildren.

Jacques Stroumsa, Jerusalem

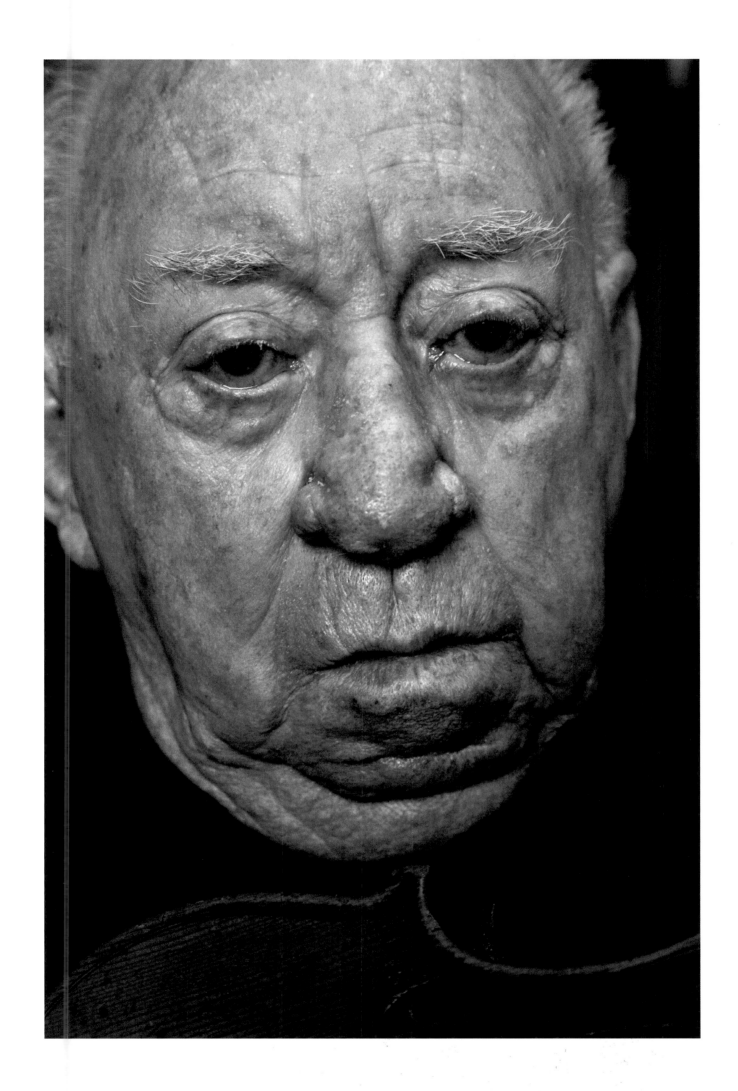

Laura and Jacques Stroumsa in their home in Jerusalem

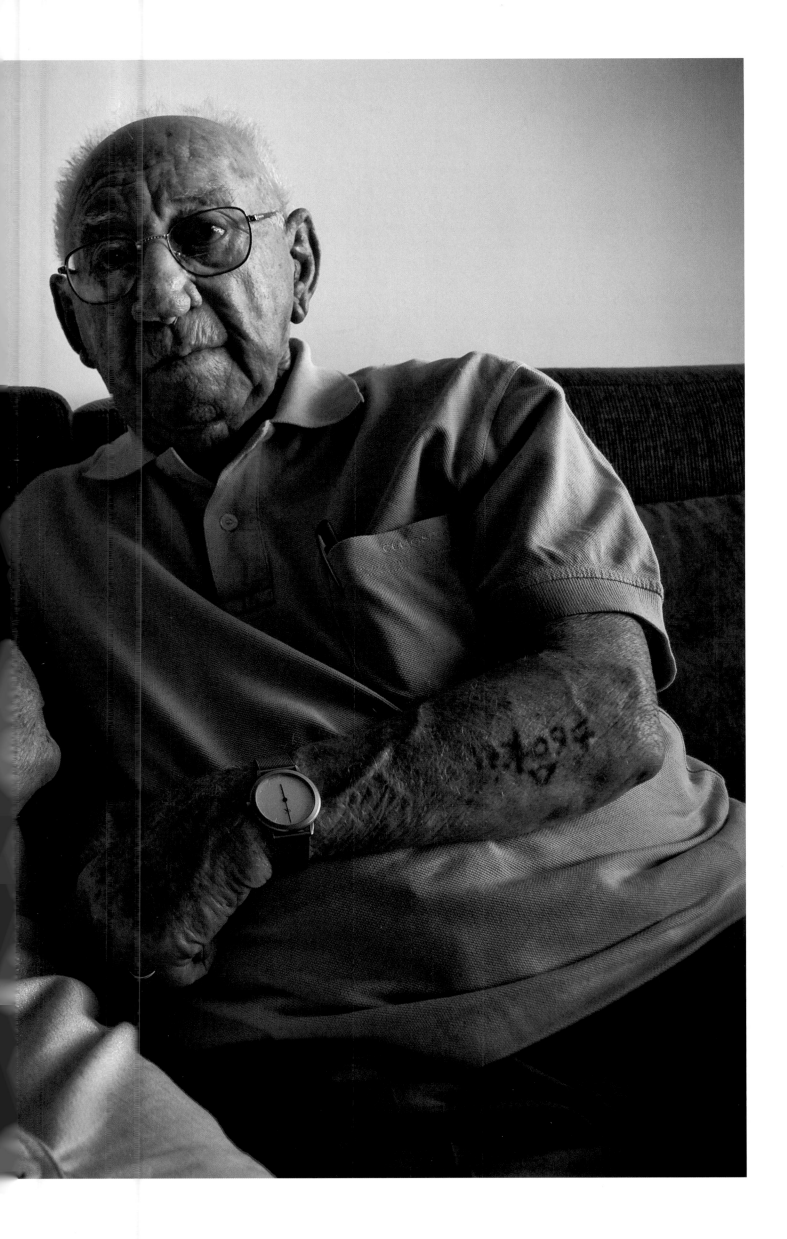

The Stroumsa family at their daughter's home, Tzur Hadassah

Uri Orlev – Poland

Uri Orlev, born in 1931, grew up in an assimilated Jewish family in Warsaw. When the Second World War broke out, his father was sent to the front as a reserve doctor and officer in the Polish army.

Orlev and his little brother stay with their mother. In November 1940, Orlev and his brother move with their mother into the Warsaw ghetto. On June 22, 1942, the liquidation of the ghetto population starts. The two children move with their mother to a factory that is producing for the Germans. On September 16, 1942, Orlev (without his brother) is caught with his mother and sent from the factory to the holding area from where the Jews are sent to Treblinka. The two of them manage to escape.

On August 13, 1942, the two children are smuggled out of the ghetto to the Polish side of the city. They are caught; however, at the last moment some German officer prevents their deaths at the hands of two plainclothes Gestapo agents, and orders them to be sent to a death camp. Contact is made with their mother. The three of them arrive at the dispatch area and run away.

September 27, 1942, their mother falls ill, partially paralyzed, and is hospitalized at the Jewish Hospital. On January 18, 1943, the patients and doctors from the hospital are sent to a death camp. The patients who are unable to get up and walk to the train are shot in their beds. Their aunt, Stephanya, adopts the two children.

On February 4, 1943, the two are smuggled out of the ghetto a second time. They hide with Polish families. On July 13, 1943, the children travel on a regular train with their aunt to Germany to be exchanged for Germans from Palestine. They arrive in Bergen-Belsen, where they are imprisoned for twenty-two months. Of a group of 1,800 only 350 remain alive.

In April 1945, they are sent by train from the camp, traveling eastward with the survivors of their group and people from another camp. On April 13, all aboard the train are liberated by the US Army, which clears out for them a residential area in the small town of Hillersleben, near Magdeburg. When it becomes clear that the area will be handed over to the Soviets, most of the refugees flee to Belgium.

In September 1945, their aunt attaches the two boys to a large group of refugees from Bergen-Belsen, and they are transported by the Jewish Brigade to Marseille. On September 9, 1945, the children travel by themselves on a Canadian ship to Palestine and are adopted by Kibbutz Genigar.

Orlev did his military service in the infantry and Nachal, after which he returned to be a member of Genigar, married and had a first daughter, Lee. He worked in the cowshed and started to write. He remarried in 1964, and had three children, Daniella, Itamar and Michael. Orlev lives in Jerusalem. He is grandfather to four grandchildren: Elia, seventeen, and Shaul, twelve, the children of Lee; Rio, four, and Amitai, eight months, the children of Daniella.

At first Orlev wrote for adults and published three books. *Lead Soldiers*, *Till Tomorrow*, and *Last Summer Vacation*. Since 1976 he has written mainly for children and youth, and to date has published thirty-one books. His books have been translated into thirty-five languages. He has received over forty prizes in Israel and abroad, and he was the first Israeli author to win the Hans Christian Andersen Gold Medal, in 1996. Orlev translates literature from Polish into Hebrew and meets many young students of various ages, high school students and teachers in schools in Israel and around the world.

"At one of the meetings I particularly remember," he recounts, "I met with fifth-grade children in Berlin. The students asked, 'How do you feel to come to Germany?'

"I told them how at the time of the liquidation of the ghetto, seeing the atrocities that were occurring, an adult who was standing next to me says, 'Yurek, you're a child, perhaps you'll survive the war. Remember after the war to take revenge on the Germans.' Then I told the children that in my first year in the Land of Israel, when I was a student at school, I used to keep an atom bomb under my bed, and sometimes, before I fell asleep, I thought whether I should throw my bomb on Berlin, the city of evil, or not.

"A little girl put up her hand and asked, 'Did you throw it?'

"I stayed quiet for a moment, then said, 'No. I thought that in Berlin there were also children like me and like my little brother, and mothers like our mother.'

"There was silence. The girl said, 'Thank you.'"

Uri Orlev, Jerusalem 2008

46   A playing card folded into an envelope

A lock of his mother's hair, cut off by Uri on her deathbed and kept in the card envelope ever since 47

48   The wooden truck and soldiers with which Uri played during the war. They were donated to the Artifacts Department of the Yad Vashem Holocaust Martyrs' and Heroes' Remembrance Authority in 2007.

Two generals and a secret advisor (on hiding places): colored rolls of wood on which Uri painted faces, and with which he played in the cellar in the village where he was hidden. They were donated to the Artifacts Department of the Yad Vashem Holocaust Martyrs' and Heroes' Remembrance Authority in 2007.

The Orlev family, Jerusalem

Chava M. Dinner-Loopuit – Holland

I was born on November 14, 1937, in Amsterdam. My mother was Chana Rothschild and my father Bernard Loopuit, from an old Dutch Jewish family. My mother was a refugee from Germany who came to Holland with her parents and her younger sister in 1933 and was also a member of the Pioneer Training program in northern Holland, organized by Bachad (the Covenant of Religious Pioneers). My parents married in 1936. My father had two married brothers and an elderly mother, my grandmother. My maternal grandmother lived with us in our home. I studied in a Montessori preschool. In the area where we lived there were a lot of Jews, mainly young families. A large, modern synagogue was built near our house.

In 1942 the expulsions to the extermination camps began and the situation deteriorated badly. My parents considered hiding my sister and me. Every so often they got deferrals of their expulsion (*Sperre*) in the form of a stamp on their identity cards. My aunt had contacts in the underground that dealt with hiding Jews, and she found them a hiding place; however, my father refused and my mother did what he did. At the beginning of 1943, my mother prepared me for the possibility of leaving home and traveling to somewhere far off until they "came to take me back." Since I had seen the expulsions from the window of our house, with adults and children with backpacks clambering onto trucks, I understood the danger we were in and didn't voice any opposition. I was promised that my sister would also be sent to a similar place.

On March 12, 1943, I parted from my parents. They stayed in control of their emotions while they were with me, and handed me over with a bag full of clothes, books and toys to a volunteer from the underground. The journey took hours, and I only reached the family in the evening, in a village in northern Holland, in the province of Friesland. The head of the family was a key member of the underground in the area. After a couple of days he took me to the place intended for me, the home of his mother-in-law in the neighboring village. She was a woman of sixty, the mother of seven grown-up children, at home and away from home. An unmarried daughter of thirty-two was the one who mainly looked after me. The grandmother reminded me of my own grandma and I loved her.

It was very difficult for me to get used to the customs and the mentality. They also poked fun at my accent, but in general their attitude toward me was good. They made sure I had clothes and toys and also received teaching at home, because it was forbidden for me to go to school. I could only go out occasionally to the fields, accompanied by the aunty, and that was mainly toward the end when the danger had lessened. There were hiding places inside the house: in the attic, on the second floor between the walls, and also underneath the house, which was built on pillars. I recall one particularly difficult day when the Germans came to round up young men for forced labor; whoever ran away was shot. Two sons of the family were taken. Not all the slave laborers returned from Germany; one son died, the other came back. The grandmother also died in the final months of the war. The aunt was left alone in the house and I was with her, until November 1945, about half a year after the end of the war, when I was eight. She did everything she could to keep me with her, but because she did not have a husband, the Dutch authorities would not allow it. I kept in close contact with her until I made aliyah. After that we corresponded. She visited Israel once, and I visited her twice. She passed away in 1972.

Those [family members] who survived the Shoah were my father's oldest brother, his wife and daughter; the younger sister of my mother and my mother's older brother, who had moved to Palestine in 1938; my sister also survived. After the war we met but we did not go back to growing up together. Following a ruling by the Dutch court that dealt with war orphans and with the agreement of the uncles, it was decided to put me in the children's home in the city of Hilversum, which had a religious-Zionist educational orientation. I went to the public school in the city from third grade.

In 1949 I made aliyah to Israel. I lived with my uncle in Tel Aviv, where I went to elementary school, after which to high school and teachers' training college. When I graduated in 1956 I married my husband, whom I had met a year and a half earlier. We moved to the Negev at the beginning of 1957. We were both teachers. There our children were born, two sons, a daughter and then twin girls.

We moved to Jerusalem in 1967; I studied at the university for a bachelor's degree in education, literature and Hebrew language. After a few years I continued my studies for a master's in education and Jewish studies, which I completed in 1982. That same year I started studies in librarianship and information management. Since then I have worked in librarianship and bibliographies. My children got married in the years 1980–1985 and they all have children of their own, all of whom live in Israel.

Since 1988 I have visited Holland each year to be with my sister. She has visited Israel three times, in 1961, 2000 and 2007. In 2000 we all went (thirty-two of us, including daughters-in-law and sons-in-law) on a roots trip to Holland for nine days. When I retired, I took on volunteering work: one day a week in the Zionist archives, and I organize social and cultural activities for the Jerusalem branch of the Organization of Dutch Olim.

Chava Dinner, Jerusalem

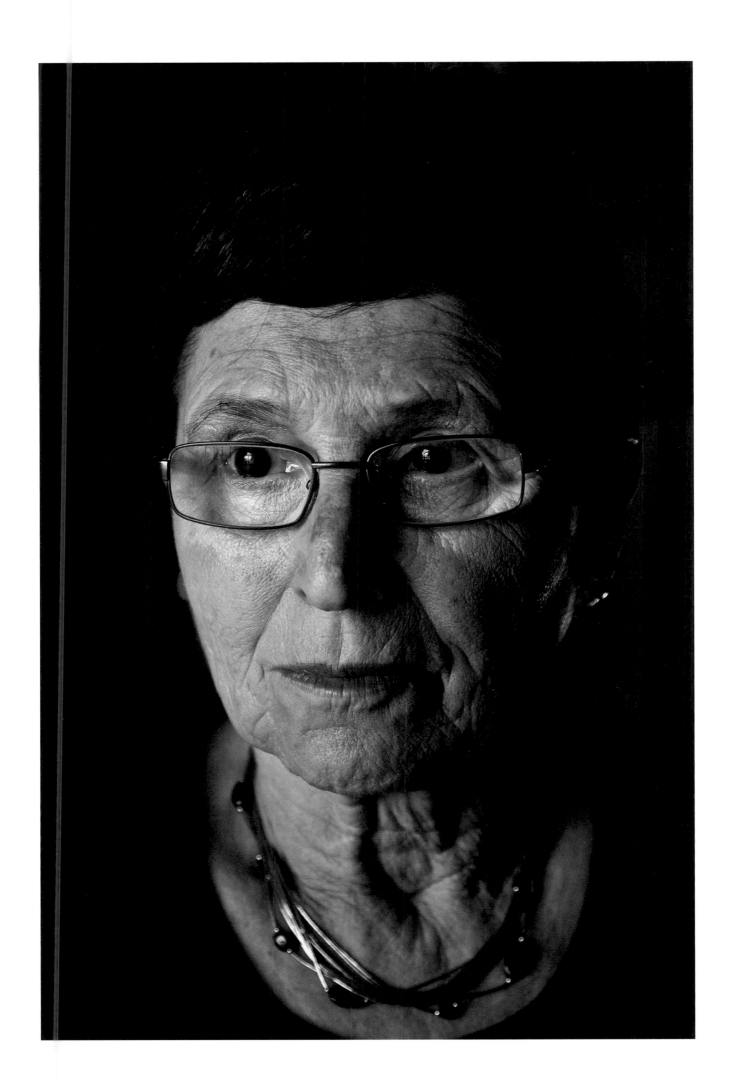

The jewel necklace given to Chava's mother by her father on the occasion of their wedding in October 1936. It was returned to Chava after the war.

The tea set from her parents' home, which was preserved in an unknown place and returned to Chava after the war

The Dinner family in Ofra

Sabina Schweid – Poland

I was born in 1931 in Zborov, a little town in Galicia. My parents, Yannek and Yunka Fuchs, were well-to-do by the standards of our town. My father was a trader and my mother was a qualified pharmacist, though she preferred to keep the firm's books. I had a particularly happy childhood. We had beautiful toys that father brought back from his business trips to Lvov or Cracow. I had lovely books with colored illustrations. In the vacations we went up to the Carpathian Mountains, renting a house and spending two months there... In a nutshell, I had everything a child could want.

My parents were Zionists, and from childhood I heard from them about the Land of Israel and their wish that I build my life there. When I was four my father organized a group of children into a Jewish preschool, and in that way I was able to study until second grade in a "cultural" institution where we learned, apart from Hebrew, the culture and ideals of the Zionist movement. I have no doubt that my parents' home and the preschool of Mr. Yavetz, my first teacher, determined to a great extent my path in life.

When the Second World War broke out in 1939, I was a girl of eight, and everything was taken away in one go. The Russian army overran our town. Our house was confiscated by the Soviet authorities and was shared out between us and four families of functionaries brought in from Russia. Father's trading house was also expropriated, and as a Zionist-bourgeois family we were in danger of being sent to Siberia. Yet despite all this, my parents managed to maintain a family and cultural setting, and to celebrate the Jewish festivals. I continued to learn Hebrew with a private teacher and I even befriended our Russian neighbors. However, in the summer of 1941, the Molotov-Ribbentrop Pact was broken and the Germans invaded Zborov.

After a heavy bombardment by the Luftwaffe I was sent to buy bread. I saw a man fall dead and the soldier who had fired the shot. I understood that now all the rules had changed. When I got back home and told my father, who had been an officer in the Austrian army in the First World War, what I saw, he refused to believe me. For me that was a formative moment, when I instantly grew up and realized that life had changed and would never be the same, and that I had to take responsibility. This was called by the Germans the first *Aktion* or roundup, in which only the men were murdered. In the autumn of 1941 the Jews were herded into the ghetto, where we lived in a tiny, miserable room with my aunt, whose husband had already been murdered.

When they started talking about another roundup in which the elderly and the children would be killed, my mother found a hiding place for me and my aunt at Mr. Bigus, a colorful character who was addicted to vodka. He was prepared to hide us in a pit he had dug under the barn attached to his house. In 1942, after a further *Aktion*, my parents moved to the *Lager*, a labor camp in Zborov itself. In 1943 my father was murdered, tortured to death for being accused of organizing a revolt. Since none of his friends were shot, it was clear that Father didn't give any of his friends away. My mother, another aunt and three cousins joined us in the pit of Mr. Bigus. Seven of us lived at his expense.

The town's priest introduced a Polish woman to my mother, and after he provided me and one of my cousins with Polish birth certificates, she took us and Mother in. We stayed with her under false identities for about half a year until the Red Army conquered Galicia up to the River San. We were all saved. Also the family that was in hiding at Mr. Bigus.

I was fourteen years old.

In 1945 my mother and I left on our way to Palestine. We sneaked onto trains, got across borders, crawled out at night from the train that had become our home to steal apples and carrots from the fields, because we didn't have any food. At that age, everything appeared to me like one big adventure.

We reached Duggendorf, a refugee camp in Bavaria, where we waited with the few survivors to make aliyah. Moshe, a survivor like me, taught me Bialik's poems, and Zvi told me about the Magdiel agricultural school, which he described as though it was paradise. As a fifteen-year-old girl I obtained a certificate, and so arrived in Palestine with a small group of young people, quite legally. I tried to come with Aliyah Bet, but its ship, the *Bracha Fold,* was caught and sent to Cyprus. It would only reach Israel in 1948. I arrived before it, in April 1946.

I was sent by Youth Aliyah to the Ayanot agricultural school. Apart from agricultural knowledge, this school gave me an education in labor movement values. I learned to take pleasure not just from the fruits of my work, but also from the effort itself that I invested in it.

In time I became a teacher of art history, and I still enjoy studying and teaching.

I married Eli Schweid, whom I met during my military

service, in Jerusalem in 1953. The family we built is the center of my life and my biggest achievement. We helped each other to grow and to develop; we brought up three children, two daughters and a son. We have five grandsons and five granddaughters. All are good people, educated, providing for their families honorably and raising their children properly.

We have many joyful occasions and *nachat* [pleasure] from our family, as well as some moments of pain, as in every family. Our home is a traditional one.

I know my parents would have been proud of me and my family.

As to myself, I consider myself lucky. Now in my old age, my life passes before me like the beads of an amber necklace. Some burnt pieces have been preserved, but also some delicate threads of lace. There are days of fun and days of pain. But everything was covered by time with a transparent, burnt but glittering layer. To all of which has been added the brilliant sparkles of a dream come true.

Sabina Schweid, Jerusalem

Challah cover, handmade by Sabina's grandmother

A homemade diary in the rabbi's handwriting. Sabina's mother marked the date of the *Aktion*, April 9, 1943, with a purple pen.

[pp. 66–67] The hole in the blanket was caused by embers buried in the ground underneath where Sabina slept, in an attempt to overcome the cold

The Schweid family in Jerusalem

Dina Kol – Hungary

I was born in the town of Nyíregyháza, Hungary, in 1928 to the late Elona Hannah née Halpert and the late Sandor Shimon Friedman. Both were murdered very young in Auschwitz. Mother was forty-one and Father was forty-five.

The town of my birth had about fifty thousand inhabitants, of whom about five thousand were Jews. My parents were members of the Orthodox community and were very punctilious in the performance of religious commandments. Yet my father was educated and very well informed about what was happening in the world, loved literature, read a great deal, but did not neglect to learn Gamara from time to time. As was usual in those days, my father was responsible for earning a living and my mother was a housewife (and an excellent one too!). She had a beautiful voice and the house was always filled with her singing. From my father I inherited the love of books and from my mother her voice and the love of singing. I still sing in a choir and occasionally also solo.

At home we were two daughters, my sister Ahuva and I – she was three years older than me. We had a small brother, the "*Kaddishel*" [the little child who one day would say Kaddish, the memorial prayer, for his parents], who died at the age of three from a serious illness, when I was six. My parents mourned him for years.

My sister and I took the same studies path: four years in the community elementary school, then we went on to the high school. Unfortunately, I was unable to complete my schooling on account of the racial laws against the Jews. When I was thirteen my parents allowed me to join Hashomer Hatzair, contrary to what was accepted in the community to which my parents belonged. That was how I was exposed to a Zionist movement and to the attachment to the Land of Israel. Before I ever knew Hebrew I knew and sang songs of the Land of Israel. Those songs are etched on my memory till this very day. We were lucky enough to have a young rabbi in our town, Dr. Wachs, who started to teach us Hebrew. He concentrated on grammar, and when I came to Israel, it was on account of him that I was able to speak Hebrew properly. To my great regret, this marvelous person was also murdered at a young age during the Shoah. I will always remember him.

The day after the German invasion on February 17, 1944, we were obliged to wear the yellow star and were herded together in the ghetto. At the end of May 1944, we were loaded onto cattle wagons for the journey to Auschwitz. The train hurtled crazily for three days and three nights straight to Auschwitz. There we lost our parents and our humanity was stolen from us. My sister and I went through the terrible period in Auschwitz, in the shadow of the crematoria, and in the neighboring concentration camp, Dachau-Kaufring, each one looking after and encouraging the other.

The hoped-for and long-awaited liberation came after a death march that lasted two weeks. We were liberated on May 1, 1945. After recovering at a displaced persons camp, we looked for ways to get to Palestine. It never occurred to us to return to Hungary.

At the Feldafing displaced persons camp we joined a new group, the United Pioneer Youth, which was getting organized to go to Palestine. There I met my husband Osca, and after a short time, on May 15, 1946, we got married, before I was even eighteen. It turned out that my choice was the right one, because sixty-two years have passed and we live happily and have brought up a large, lovely family. The first great-grandson will very shortly be celebrating his bar mitzvah.

We arrived in Palestine in May 1947, on a small, dilapidated refugee ship, the *Latrun*. Off the coast of Palestine we were caught by a British warship and obliged to surrender. We were expelled to Cyprus.

We were again imprisoned behind barbed wire, and again soldiers were guarding us, just one year after we had been released from a concentration camp. The seven months on Cyprus passed with me pregnant, under very difficult conditions. But those difficult conditions on Cyprus did not prevent many young couples from starting families. When the British realized that there was going to be a serious problem – the camps of course were not ready for childbirth and certainly not for bringing up babies – they decided to send the women in advanced pregnancy to Palestine. There we were imprisoned in Atlit and there I gave birth to my first daughter, a present for my nineteenth birthday. When Hannele was eight days old, a friend from Kibbutz Afikim came and took us "home," our first and last home since then. After a short while, my husband Osca, together with the whole group, joined us.

Three months later the disturbances started and the War of Independence broke out. Since the Jordan Valley had become the front line, the mothers and all the children were evacuated to Haifa, where we spent several months. Osca transported food to besieged Jerusalem.

Throughout my life I worked in the education system. When the children had grown up, I had the time, at age fifty-seven, to complete my high school studies, which I did, to my great surprise, with distinction.

Despite the happiness of our lives, the memory of the Shoah still accompanies us. We remember and we continue to tell about it. We have sixteen grandchildren and six great-grandchildren. Our hope is that our children will be able to bring up theirs in peace and tranquility. Please let it be so!

Dina Kol, Kibbutz Afikim

Osca Kol (Kolodowsky) – Lithuania

I was born on April 18, 1925, in Kovno, Lithuania, to Tanya née Bergson and Meir Kolodowsky. (We Hebraized the name after the birth of our second son.)

I obtained my general and Zionist education in my parents' home, in the Youth Movement and the Schwab Hebrew Gymnasium [high school], where I studied from preschool age until the completion of my studies in 1941. My childhood and the beginning of my youth were spent in the bosom of my loving family that cared for every need. While my father brought in the livelihood and looked after our well-being, my mother spoiled us and was the leader. From her I got my love of reading, of which in those days I could not get enough. In school we were in a kind of bubble, cut off from the antisemitism that ruled the outside world. After the Molotov-Ribbentrop Pact, Lithuania was overrun by the Red Army and Poland fell to Germany.

In June 1940 Lithuania became the sixteenth Soviet Republic, and at a single stroke our world changed. All the Jewish institutions, which had been part of community life for generations, were closed down and broken up. It was also the end for all parts of the Zionist movement. With the guidance of my previous youth movement leaders, I started underground activity to maintain the Hebrew language and the bond with Zion. Some of the members, myself included, managed to save from the flames part of the Hebrew library that was kept in a cupboard in the staff room.

On June 22, 1941, planes of the *Luftwaffe* attacked the town at the beginning of Operation Barbarossa, to conquer the Soviet Union. Before the arrival of the German army, a Lithuanian mob broke into the homes of Jews and a dreadful slaughter started that lasted three days. In Kovno seven thousand Jews were slaughtered. In a deadly fury, seven hundred years of good neighborliness were sundered in one go, and most of Lithuania's Jews were murdered.

By chance death passed me and my family by. We were herded with the rest of the survivors into the ghetto, and fate had earmarked us for suffering and degradation, hard labor, malnutrition, disease and roundups. We were engaged in a desperate war for survival every single hour of the day, every moment, to retain the remnants of our humanity, using every sliver of hope to remain a human being in an inhuman situation. What my father said to strengthen our resolve was, "*Kindrelach, mir wollen sei eriberleben*" (Children, we want to survive). In one of the roundups they also took my mother, who was murdered at the Ninth Fort. She was forty-six when she was killed.

I joined the resistance, and at night I dug bunkers to hide during the roundups that we knew were coming. The ghetto was razed before I managed to join the partisans.

When the Soviet army was already 100 km from the city, the Germans decided to expel the remainder of the Jews of Kovno to Germany. We went into the bunker but were discovered and joined the rest of those expelled. The ghetto went up in fire, and many died in the flames.

On July 14, 1944, we were loaded onto freight trains for the journey to Germany. In Germany I passed through four concentration camps, of which the last was Dachau. My father died on April 8, 1945, on the wet shower floor. With his head on my knees I saw how the last drop of life was squeezed out of his suffering body, swollen from hunger. With his death I lost the support that had helped me survive till then. As the front approached, they took out of Dachau all those who were still strong enough to stand on their feet in a march toward the Bavarian Alps. It was still winter in the Alps, and the march became a death march. Many died of cold or were shot along the route of the march.

On April 30, 1945, the Nazi guards vanished. Several friends and I started to move in the direction we had come from, and on May 1, 1945, we were liberated by an American armored unit. A few days later I came down with typhus and meningitis. I was lucky to be brought, unconscious, by my friends to the American hospital in Garmisch. Thanks to the diligent care and new medicines, I remained alive.

When I had recovered I reached the Feldafing displaced persons camp, and together with other friends from Lithuania we set up the United Youth Halutz movement, with a view to organize youth groups for agricultural training and aliyah. In the movement's club house I met Dina, a survivor from Hungary, who married me on May 15, 1946. Despite the limitations on aliyah made by the British, we set out as illegal immigrants. We were stopped on the high seas by British warships, and were imprisoned as illegal immigrants at the holding camp in Cyprus for seven months. In July 1947 we eventually reached our new home in Afikim, with Dina clasping our eldest daughter, Hannele, who was born in the Atlit prison camp.

When the country quieted down, I was called up to the regular army, and I became one of the founders of the Nachal [combined army and settlement of the land]. I left the army with the rank of captain, as a company commander in the infantry. On my release I joined the banana industry, where I stayed almost until the age of eighty.

Life was good to us: we were blessed with a happy home, love and friends. Despite this and all the happiness we had, the shadow of the past will accompany me to the end of my days.

Osca Kol, Kibbutz Afikim

Osca with *The Scream*, a stained glass statue he made

Dina and Osca Kol in their home on Kibbutz Afikim

The Kol family in the Jerusalem Forest

Yoshua Tessler – Romania

I was born in Cluj in 1921 to Sheindel-Yaffa Moskovitz and Yirmiyahu Tessler. My family was involved in the production and sale of wines and spirits. We dressed European style, but we were students and followers of Rav Yoel, the Satmar Rebbe.

In 1940, after the fall of France and the Vienna Awards, Transylvania was handed over as a prize to Hungary, which was an ally of Germany. The Hungarian government was antisemitic, implementing anti-Jewish laws.

In 1942 I became engaged to Ester (Elisabeth Helman). Her family owned one of the largest bakeries in Cluj. The head of the family had received a professional award from the king of Romania, which led to harassment by the Hungarian authorities against him and his bakery.

On March 19, 1943, in the cellar of our house, which was a storeroom for raw materials for distilling spirits, my family hid our volumes of Gemara (which had been bought by my father as separate sheets printed by the Vilna Press, and which were later bound in leather by a master binder in our town), various household articles and clothes. The entry to the cellar was sealed with cement.

On May 3, 1944, the family moved to the ghetto of Cluj. Life in the ghetto was hell. It was located in the area of a brick factory. Each family received four square meters [thirteen square feet] to live in. Water was brought in buckets from outside the ghetto. There were communal lavatories in the form of a cesspit right at the end of the ghetto. The result was that a month later under these very poor conditions, everyone signed up willingly to leave for Auschwitz, on the assumption that it couldn't be worse.

On June 5, 1944, the entire family was sent to Auschwitz. After a week they moved my father, Reb Yirmiyahu Tessler, and me to the Kaufring labor camp in Bavaria. My paternal and maternal grandmothers, Mother's younger brother and sisters, the uncles and aunts on my father's side, together with their children, were all sent to the gas chambers.

In July 1944 a group of Jews who had survived the liquidation of the Kovno ghetto arrived at the Kaufring camp. Because of the speed of the expulsion, the members of the group arrived with a few personal belongings and in civilian dress. (That is to say, they did not come through Auschwitz, their personal belongings were not taken from them and they were not wearing prisoners' clothing.)

At my father's instigation, I inquired of one of the "newcomers" – his name was Abramowitz, may the Lord avenge his spilled blood (he didn't survive) – if perhaps someone had a pair of tefillin [phylacteries]. Abramowitz answered that he would ask around. If we managed to meet the next day, he would give me an answer. The next day we met. Yes, there is a pair of tefillin, whose parchment and boxes had been prepared underground in the Kovno ghetto. The owner was prepared to sell them. If we managed to meet the next day, they would do the deal. The next day we met. The deal took place. My father and I bought the tefillin for our daily food ration, two slices of bread.

The tefillin served my father and me until the end of the war, with dozens of people putting them on when the occasion permitted, most not out of any religious sentiments, and said *Shema Yisrael* [Hear O Israel, the Jewish declaration of faith]; or some would just watch as others put them on, obviously all in secret, with someone always guarding the entrance to the hut. This act constituted a sort of expression of our humanity, which we endeavored to preserve.

In April 1945 the US Army liberated us at Alch, near Dachau.

After a lot of wandering and with the involvement of the Jewish Brigade, we reached a camp near Venice. There I received a message that my fiancée had also survived and returned with what was left of her family to Cluj. I returned to Cluj and we married on August 12, 1945. At the wedding I wore a suit that had been kept in the cellar. The volumes of Gemara and household articles also remained intact.

In 1948 our oldest daughter, Annette-Zippora, was born in Cluj.

In September 1958 we made aliyah to Israel. We joined my father, Yirmiyahu, who had already come to Israel in 1950 and lived in Jerusalem. We hadn't received permission from the Romanian authorities to move to Israel together with my father.

In Jerusalem he had set up the Atas soft drinks factory. I joined the business and worked with my father in the factory.

In 1959 our younger daughter, Rachel, was born.

In 1969 our older daughter married Shai Luria, of blessed memory, who had been born in Yavne'el, was a member of Kibbutz Tirat Tzvi and his family had been five generations in the Land of Israel.

In 1973 our younger daughter married Jacob Chalamish, who had been born in the country and was a member of Kibbutz Ein HaNatziv, the son of parents from Germany who came to Palestine in 1933.

In all we have had twelve grandchildren and five great-grandchildren.

I retired in 1991. When my wife became sick, I took on myself to deal with all the housework. She passed away on February 13, 2006.

I continue to be active in my synagogue, to study in *chavrutot* with learning partners, and to take pleasure from my family.

Yoshua Tessler, Jerusalem

[pp. 82–83] Tefillin made underground in the Kovno ghetto and sold to Yoshua and his father for two daily portions of bread

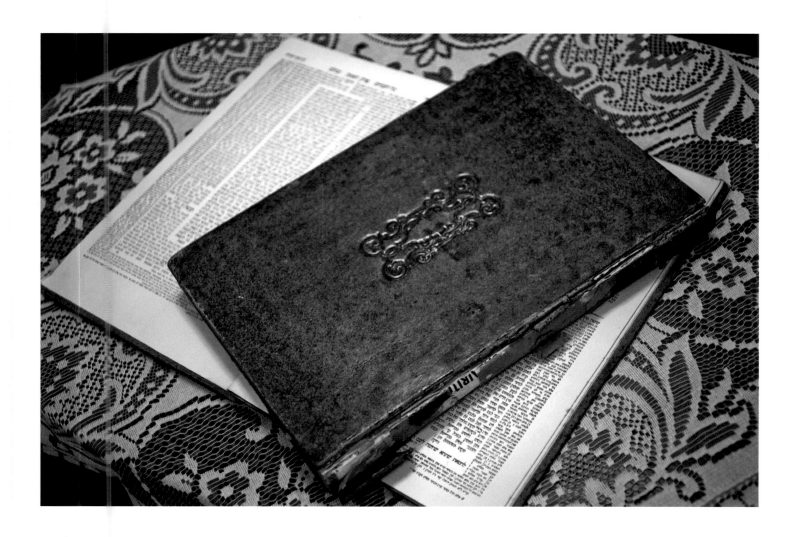

Volumes of the Gemara hidden in the cellar – whose entrance was sealed with cement – and found intact after the war

The Tessler family, Jerusalem

[pp. 90–91] Torah scrolls saved from destroyed Jewish communities in Europe

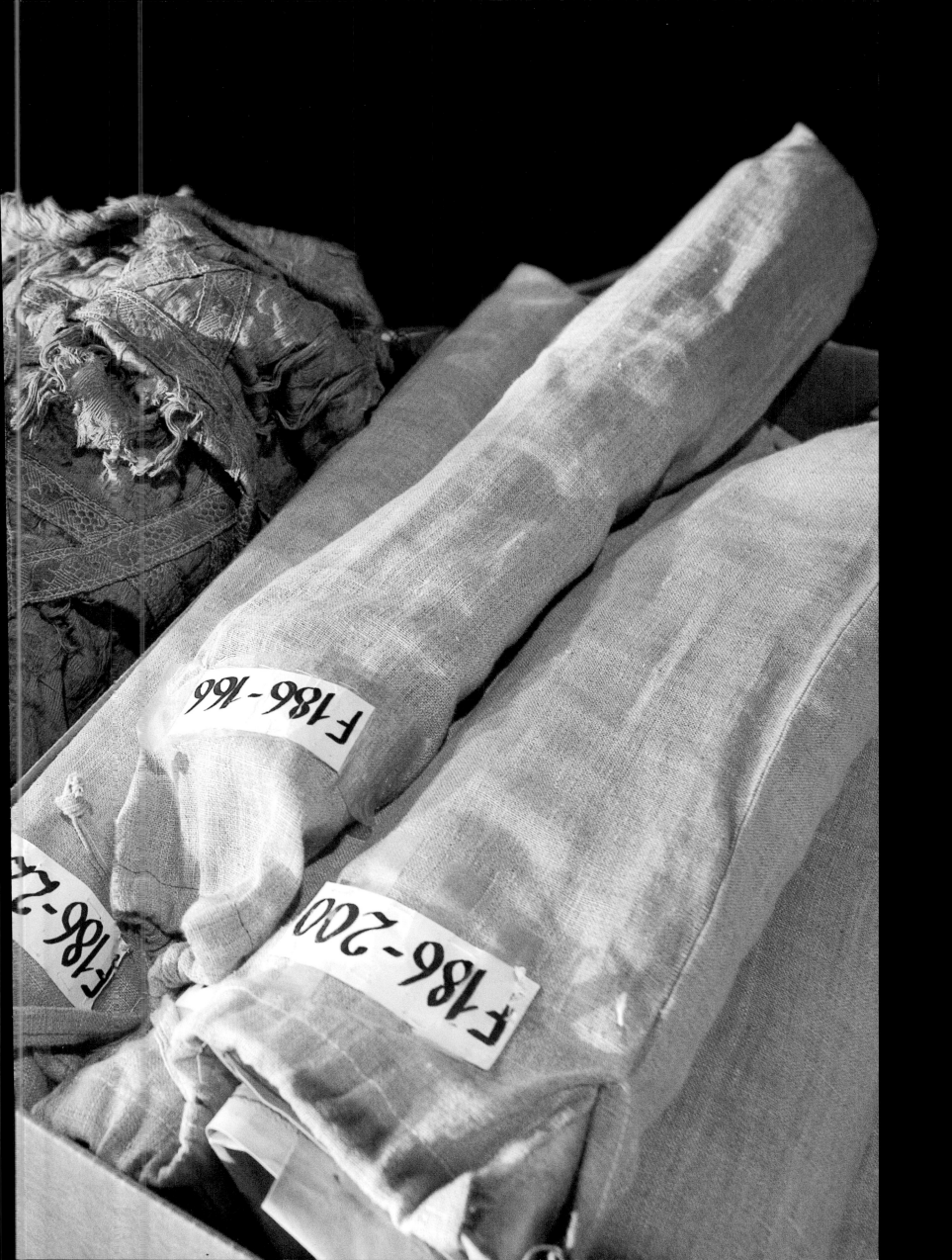

Genia Kowalski – Poland

Genia was born in Pabianice on March 7, 1919. Her father was Hilmeier-Gelbart and her mother was Esther-Leah née Friedman. The parents moved to live in Brzeziny, where her sister Hilda was born. Two-year-old Genia was sent to live with her grandmother and her family because of her father's illness; he died when she was four years old. Her mother remarried to Chanina Zwerin. After her brother was born, Genia was returned to her home. When the war broke out her brother was four.

Immediately following the Nazi conquest, her mother was murdered by the Nazis when she returned from the village and dollars were found on her body. Her stepfather died immediately upon the arrival of the Germans, and the three children were left orphans. In 1940 the three of them were placed in the Brzeziny ghetto.

In 1942 her little brother was torn from her arms and was taken, together with other children and their mothers; they were taken in closed trucks to their deaths. She was sent by train, but someone took her out from the death transport. In April 1942 she was transferred to the Lodz ghetto with her sister. Ten families lived together in a single small room. Genia was sent to work as a seamstress in a clothing factory for German soldiers.

Genia was in the Lodz ghetto until 1944. In August of that year she was sent to Auschwitz after she was caught out in the street. In Auschwitz she met up again with her sister, who had been sent there a bit before. The meeting was very hard, because it was only when she saw her sister that she understood how much she had deteriorated. In Auschwitz she became sick with typhoid fever, though her life was saved by her Kapo: when she saw she was sick, she left her in the hut and put a whole pile of blankets on top of her. The German who came in to check jabbed the blankets with his bayonet, but miraculously did not strike her. In the evening when they took off the blankets, everyone was amazed to see her in one piece and even healthy. Her sister did not enjoy the same good luck and was burnt alive with her entire hut after a case of typhus was discovered there.

She was sent with a group of five hundred girls to the gas chambers, but at the last moment was taken out. The reason is unclear to this day. They were moved to Berlin, to the Ravensbruck women's camp, where she worked in a Krupp weapons factory until the spring of 1945.

On April 15, 1945, she was transferred to Sweden as part of the deal made with Himmler.

She was the only survivor from her entire extended family (apart from three distant relatives). She was treated in Sweden and found asylum there. There she met Tzvi Kowalski, whom she married in 1948.

When they reached Israel in 1949, they lived in a *ma'abara*, a refugee camp, where Genia refused to stay. They were offered a house in Jaffa, but Genia was not prepared to live in that luxurious Arab house either, because she realized the residents had fled, and all their property, even their food, had been left behind in the house. They went to live in an orange warehouse in Nachlat Yehuda, near Rishon LeZion, where their eldest daughter was born.

Tzvi was an electrical contractor and Genia a housewife. From 1956 they lived in Rishon LeZion. The couple had three daughters, six grandchildren and two great-grandchildren.

Dvora Morag, her daughter

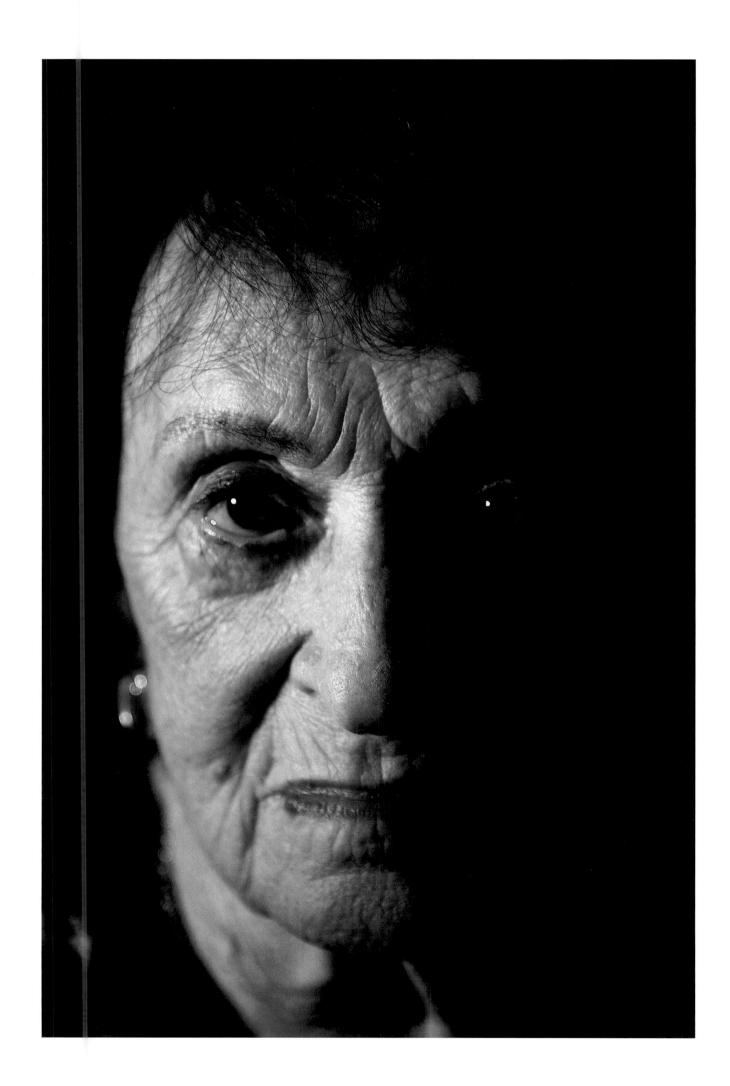

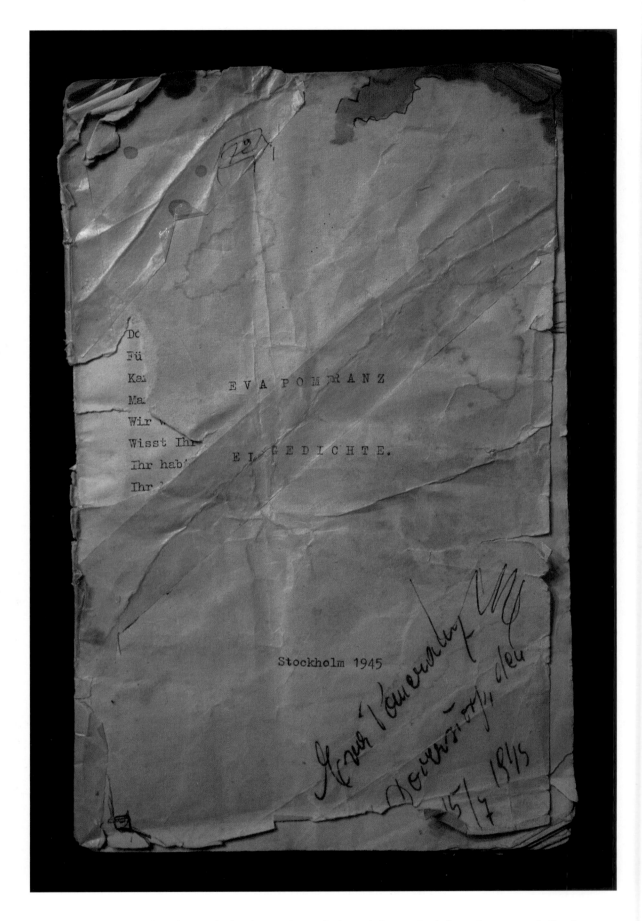

94   Booklet of poetry of a refugee who lost her son in Auschwitz and given to Genia in a refugee camp in Sweden

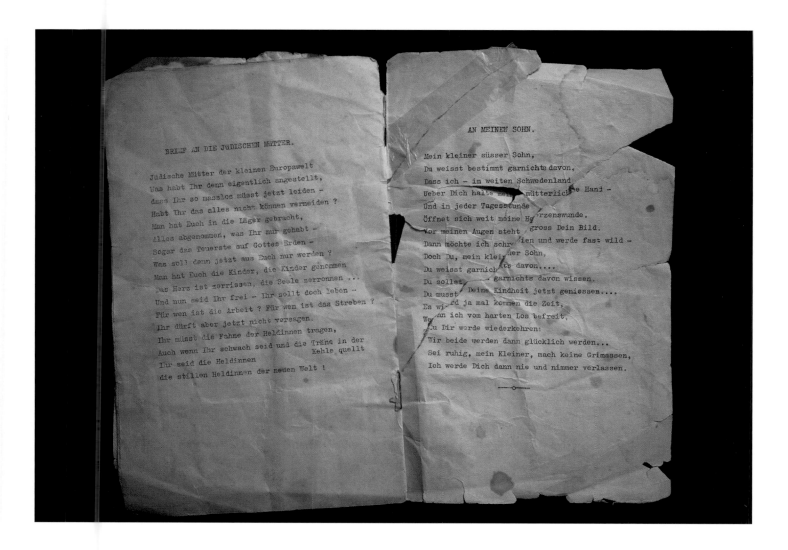

Translation of left-hand page:

Letter to Jewish Mothers

Jewish mothers of the little world of Europe, what were your crimes that brought down on you endless suffering – did you not know how to avoid all that? You were imprisoned in camps, all your belongings were taken away from you, what was dearest to you was stolen – what will be with you? Also the children, they took them too. The heart is torn. The soul has dissolved... And now you have been liberated – you should yet live – For whom to labor? For whom to make an effort? But now is not the time to retreat. Raise the banner of courage, even though you are weak and strangled with tears. You are the heroes, the quiet heroes of the new world.

Translation of right-hand page:

To My Son

My dear little son, you don't know anything about the fact that I hold you with a maternal hand in the large land of Sweden, and that every hour of the day the wound in my heart opens wide. Before my eyes I see your picture. Then I want to scream, I go crazy, and you are not aware. Indeed it's better you know nothing about it, enjoy your childhood.... The day will come when I will be freed of this harsh fate, and I will return to you: then the two of us will be happy together.... Hush, quiet, dear, don't grimace. Then I will never part from you again.

Tzvi Henryk Kowalski – Poland

He was born in Wloclawek, Poland, on November 22, 1921, to Pinchas Kowalski, who was a metal worker, and Devora née Lubinska. He had two sisters, Chana, the eldest, and Zipporah, who was younger than him.

From a very early age he was interested in electricity, which had recently arrived in Poland. In 1938 he studied for a year in a vocational school until the German invasion in 1939. The Nazis entered the town on the eve of Yom Kippur and murdered the Jews who had gathered in the synagogue. The rest were sent to the local ghetto. In 1940 the mother and daughters were sent in trucks to Lodz, according to the Germans, but afterwards it transpired that they had been murdered at Chelmno. At the beginning, father and son were sent to work in different places; his father never returned, and it was learned later on he had died of sadness and hard labor.

After Tzvi had worked as an electrician in the labor camp in the area, he was sent to the labor camp in Poznan, where they had to convert the cowsheds into places to live for the Jews sent there. In 1941 he was sent to build a railway track in Poznan and stayed there half a year. In May he was sent to Auschwitz (not Birkenau), and from there he was sent to Firstengrover camp near Auschwitz. There he worked as an electrician at the nearby coal mines. It was hard labor several hundred meters below the surface, in damp and soot. When one of the people tried to escape, the Germans shot every tenth man at the roll call.

When conditions became unbearable, they planned to escape and dug a tunnel. However, one of the people gave them away to the Germans. As a result eight of them were hung and all were made to watch. The horror stayed with him for the rest of his life.

At the end of 1944, when they closed the camp, they marched the prisoners for three full days to Geiwitz. From there they were transferred in open freight cars without food or drink in the freezing cold, many of them falling ill and dying on the way. The train brought them to a factory in Germany where they manufactured V2 rockets that the Germans used to bomb London.

A short time later, in February 1945, the camp commandant, Schmidt, received orders to exterminate the Jews, but he transferred them (about 350 Jews) in a ferry across the River Elbe to a farm owned by his father in a village near Lübeck. They worked for the villagers in order to earn some food. Tzvi repaired radios, in return for which he got food. The camp commandant heard that the Red Cross was in Lübeck and sent the Jews there. After they met the local Swedish consul (who was apparently Count Bernadotte, who had met with Himmler) they realized there was a chance they might be saved. When an American truck arrived, only western European prisoners of war were allowed to get in it. Tzvi and a friend hid under the truck, and when they climbed up introduced themselves as French and were sent to Sweden. There, in his words, he was born again, and got to know other people. They were put into a detention camp where the Swedes dealt with them, changed their clothes, washed them and fed them with extreme caution. His weight when he reached Sweden was twenty-eight kilograms [sixty-two pounds].

That of course is the dry bones of the story, just the framework. The important things are what are missing from this story, and they cannot be told.

In 1948 he married Genia, and together they moved to Israel.

Dvora Morag, his daughter

Genia and Tzvi Kowalski in their home in Rishon LeZion

The Kowalski family in Rishon LeZion

Simcha Miller – Bulgaria

I was born in 1932 in Sofia, Bulgaria, to Esther Mash and Shmuel Shmili. Our family had lived in Sofia for at least five hundred years.

My father was a Zionist and attended three Zionist Congresses. He visited Palestine frequently, as he imported lemons from there to Bulgaria. The family also visited Palestine. On one of the visits they stayed near the neighborhood of Manshia in Tel Aviv. As was the custom among the Sephardim, they were sitting in the street with the neighbors, when suddenly Arabs on horseback arrived with drawn swords and started to carry out a pogrom.

In the 1920s my parents and brothers came to Palestine for the last time. They returned to Bulgaria because my one-year-old sister became very sick. On the boat, my mother recounted, she was certain my sister had died. Fearing they would throw her body overboard, Mother hid the matter of her death. However, wonder of wonders, when they reached Bulgaria it transpired that my sister was alive, and even ate a pickled cucumber with great relish. With all their attention focused on the little sister, my parents didn't notice that my brothers had also become ill. My older brother, Herzl, died at the age of eight. They never spoke about it at home. However, on the *yahrtzeit* [anniversary of the death], my father would come home drunk.

We all went to the Hebrew preschool. We spoke a bit of Hebrew at home. Until third grade we studied Hebrew at the Jewish school. In the breaks we were obliged to speak only in Hebrew. Whoever did not speak in Hebrew received a fine: to put money in the Jewish National Fund collection box. When the Germans came, studying Hebrew was outlawed. After the war we continued to go to the Hebrew school and the teacher translated the Bible for us from Hebrew into Bulgarian.

In 1940 they took all the men aged eighteen and over to labor camps. We didn't know where the camps were, and we couldn't visit them. And they did not make visits home. We were obliged to fill out forms in which we had to waive all our rights as citizens. Decrees and prohibitions were placed on us. We were required to place a yellow star on our clothes, on the left-hand side.

My brother Shlomo took upon himself responsibility for the education at home. He gave us lessons, checked the cleanliness of our nails, etc. I was crazily attached to him.

I recall that when I was ten we took all the possessions in the house out into the street. The Jewish children stood next to stands and sold the contents of their homes. I sold embroidered tablecloths, long pillows of special satin crepe material, and other items.

The night before the expulsion we received an order to move to a town called Ruse. This was a very special town with highly cultured people. We traveled there by train. It was my first journey by train, and it was crowded and full of German soldiers. I vomited the whole way. We were scared. When we arrived, they took us in a horse-drawn cart to the Jewish school. A Jewish family took us from there to their place. At that time in Sofia there were already bombardments, but there not. There were a lot of partisans there and a large Jewish underground. The youth all started to fight the Germans, including my brother.

We all lived in the coal shed. It was only permitted to go outside for two hours a day.

My mother sewed me the yellow star under the collar so that I would be able to go out to look for work. I was ten years old. By chance I came to a macaroni factory. At the end of the day I received a bag of macaroni. That's how I started to bring in a living. My brothers worked in the grape harvest. They left and came back when it was dark so they shouldn't be caught. I used to go to the black market and exchange food items.

In Ruse there were no really poor people. If someone was short, the community would help. We were fifteen children crowded in the house, and they taught us to say, if the Gestapo came, that we had come to a birthday party. My brother was beaten a great deal by German youths. He used to return the blows. I was also beaten. When the British bombing raids started we would go down into the cellar in the freezing cold, with teeth chattering from fear and cold. My mother would give us cubes of sugar to calm us down.

After four years of living in Ruse we returned to our home in Sofia. We found a house that had been dismantled, without doors or windows. That's when the famine began. I would cry from hunger. There was no oil or bread. One day we ate beans and another day lentils. My brother Shlomo started to work in a carpentry shop. That's how things continued until 1948. For four years we slept on the floor without mattresses.

In 1948 representatives arrived from Israel, and we made aliyah.

I spent two years at Kibbutz Ramat Yochanan, until 1950. We worked half a day and we studied half a day. It was a period of great happiness. Most of the time my father worked on public works projects for the unemployed.

I always dreamed of becoming a nurse. I wanted to work in a hospital, and very much liked team work. I studied in nursing school and for many years worked at Assaf Harofeh Hospital.

I married in 1952. We had two daughters. I was happy. However, my husband was killed in a work accident. In 1966 I married my second husband, Yitzhak. Two years later I gave birth to a boy. Later on I studied cosmetics and opened up a beauty salon at home.

I have ten grandchildren and am very proud of them.

Simcha Miller, Tel Aviv

The Miller family before the henna celebration for the granddaughter, at a relative's home on Moshav Zeitan

Naomi Cassuto – France

Flashes of memory from my childhood, when I was four or five (as I have recounted to my grandchildren's school classes):

I was born in the city of Strasbourg, in northern France. In 1937, at the time of Kristallnacht, my parents fled from Germany to France. In that city a group connected to the French Jewish Scouts was formed. Tasks were divided up between members of the group. For example, it was the leader, Castor, and his wife, Pivert, who were in charge of everything that happened to us during the war years. There were soldiers, saboteurs, undercover agents, doctors and nurses, and my father, Leo, was in charge of everything to do with religion, culture and youth. He married couples, organized Pesach and wrote a very special Haggadah. He read from the Torah, taught the weekly Torah portion, and gave religious speeches.

When I was one year old the Scouts group with all their families set off on a journey that would take over five years. The journey started in northern France and ended in southern France. We traveled through forests. We slept in stables and barns of farmers along the way. We even once reached the large, beautiful chateau of the Toulouse-Lautrec family, where the children used the banisters as slides.

In the forest we were forbidden to cry or to laugh out loud. It was forbidden to shout or to sneeze loudly. It was forbidden to speak in German. That's how my mother tongue is French. Everyone wore a pendant with a fictitious name on it, though close enough to the real one. We slept in the clothes we wore. I had a blue skirt with wide shoulder straps, which I wore until it was really too small on me. They convinced me to wear it, saying that this was a scouts' uniform.

Everyone had a small beige-colored bag with a broad cord, and in it were "iron rations," especially thick cubes of chocolate. It was difficult to bite into them. There were also large, thick biscuits, which were also hard to bite. At night we slept on this bag (like battle rations for an emergency).

In the farms people gave us fresh milk from the cows and vegetables from the fields. I still remember the taste of the lovely red tomatoes. In the forests they taught us about plants, what you were allowed to eat and what was forbidden. I loved eating blackberries that grew close to the ground.

We played games that included orientation and outdoor survival skills. For example, they told us we had to find a four-leaf clover. They told us that if we found one like that it was a sign the war was over. Right up to the end of the war we looked but never found any. They taught us to climb trees. At one of the springs along the way they threw us into the deep, cold water. I actually enjoyed it and still like swimming.

All the adults had nicknames from animals or plants, which reflected their characters. The leader, Castor, was the Beaver; his wife, Pivert, well that's a bird that chirps nonstop. My father, Leo, was Lion, because most members of the group used to gather around him a lot, and he would arrange the daily program with a wide range of activities. He acted as rabbi, teacher and musician who organized the choir. My father had golden hands. When he cooked an omelet he would always toss it in the air. He also made me a doll's house out of wood from the forest that I could climb into. I spent long hours playing in it. He also used to tell wonderful exciting stories. Had he survived, my father might have decided to specialize in music. He organized choirs, and some of it was recorded and has been transferred to disks. He had a deep, beautiful voice. We heard him sing on every occasion and whistle complete tunes. He played a lot of instruments. He taught me at age four to play the recorder. Up until today I have a collection of recorders and I love playing them.

We moved from one farm to another in the direction of southern France, because the Germans were pursuing us. Most of the farmers were good people and hid us so that the Germans wouldn't find us. A few reacted very badly to children. Once I climbed up to the top of a barn and then fell into the mud near the cows. I broke my collar bone, but it healed without treatment.

We slept on the ground. For almost six years I did not know what a sheet, a blanket or pajamas were. My brother, Ariel, was born in central France. My father was caught in action and exiled to the Sahara. He also organized a choir there. He came back after a year and found his way back to us. When we reached the south of France my sister Aviva was born, just a few months before the end of the war. She is five and a half years younger than me.

My father was given the job of transferring five hundred children via Spain to Israel, and he took us north again by winding paths and roads to the border with Switzerland. The Nazis were patrolling near the border on foot and in vehicles. When they were not looking in our direction, we quickly burrowed a hole under the fence. Each of us was wrapped in a dark blanket and rolled across the border. When I untangled myself from the blanket I saw a soldier pointing his rifle at me. After a bit I understood this was a Swiss soldier. I was terribly scared. In the meantime my

mother had also rolled in her blanket together with my baby sister, and she shouted something at the soldier, who took us to the command post. We waited there a long time. Someone came up to my mother with a note. After she read it she started to cry. My brother told mother not to cry, because we would certainly meet up with our father in the Land of Israel, as he had promised. My brother apparently understood that they had caught my father.

I found out that a Jew had betrayed my father for money. They say that Castor, the leader, shot the informer. The informer had described him to the Germans as a tall man with a recorder in his back pocket. That's how the Nazis captured my father and took him with hundreds of children to Auschwitz. There he was selected to play in the orchestra that played for the victims on their way to the gas chambers. He forgot his authorization on his bed in the hut. The Kapo didn't believe him that he was an orchestra member and took him to the salt mines. No one came out of there alive. This was told to me by a man, Robert Weill, who was in the next "bed" there.

Aliyah to Israel: My mother, my brother and I came to Israel on an illegal refugee ship. We were sick with whooping cough when we set sail. We made a game of vomiting. Whoever vomited furthest won. We reached Israel but had to disembark into the sea a bit off the coast. First, we threw in the water a brown box containing the few things we had brought with us. Until today I remember how it moved further away and disappeared. Fortunately, I was holding the recorder my father had given me. When I was fifteen the recorder was taken away from me, and it has not been found since. When I lost it I felt an even greater sense of being orphaned.

When we reached the coast the British caught us and put us in the camp at Atlit in order to send us back to Europe by way of Cyprus. In the meantime they stripped everybody, women and men separately. They sprayed us with disinfectant against lice and shaved everyone's head. They threw the clothes into an enormous tank. The women went to a hut on one side through a "gate" of showers that used treated waste water, and the men went on the other side. We were dirty, sick and worn out. We were given halvah and olives. Suddenly someone called out my name and I saw a man on the other side of the fence who looked familiar. It was my Uncle Chaim, my father's oldest brother, whose smile and voice were similar to his. He stretched out his arm with a handful of colored candies in colored wrappings. This sight amazed me and I thought it was a fairy tale. The sweet taste of the candies added to the sense of heaven. I remember that my uncle, apparently to make us happy, entertained us by wiggling his ears, though an attempt at whistling didn't work.

He tried talking to us in German, which we didn't know. At that point we even recoiled from him. He was already a lawyer and managed to free us from the Atlit camp and took us to Tel Aviv, to my grandfather and grandmother (Opa and Oma). Near the house I gave the family whistle we had used when we were in the forest, in the hope of finding my father waiting for our arrival at his parents' home. Of course the whistling went unanswered. Grandpa and Grandma spoke only German. When I heard them speak, I ran in panic out of their house into the street.

Today, those of the Scouts who survived meet every year on Holocaust Memorial Day at Yad Vashem. There the names of the murdered are read out, including that of my father, Leo-Yehuda Cohen.

My husband David and I have six marvelous children: Nadav, Chanoch, Oded, Malka, Noa and Meirav; fantastic daughters-in-law and sons-in-law: Melody, Debbie, Alisa, Yuval, Yoav and Sammy; and eighteen grandchildren Guy, Shimrit, Sigalit, Shai, Eran, Keren, Re'ut, Netta, Itai, Daniel, Dana, Omri, Gali, Ro'i, Eitan and Mia.

I am a graduate of Oranim College and have a PhD from the Hebrew University, Jerusalem. After forty-one years working for the Ministry of Education teaching art the history of art, and the didactics of teaching art from primary school through to college, I am today retired.

Naomi Cassuto, Jerusalem

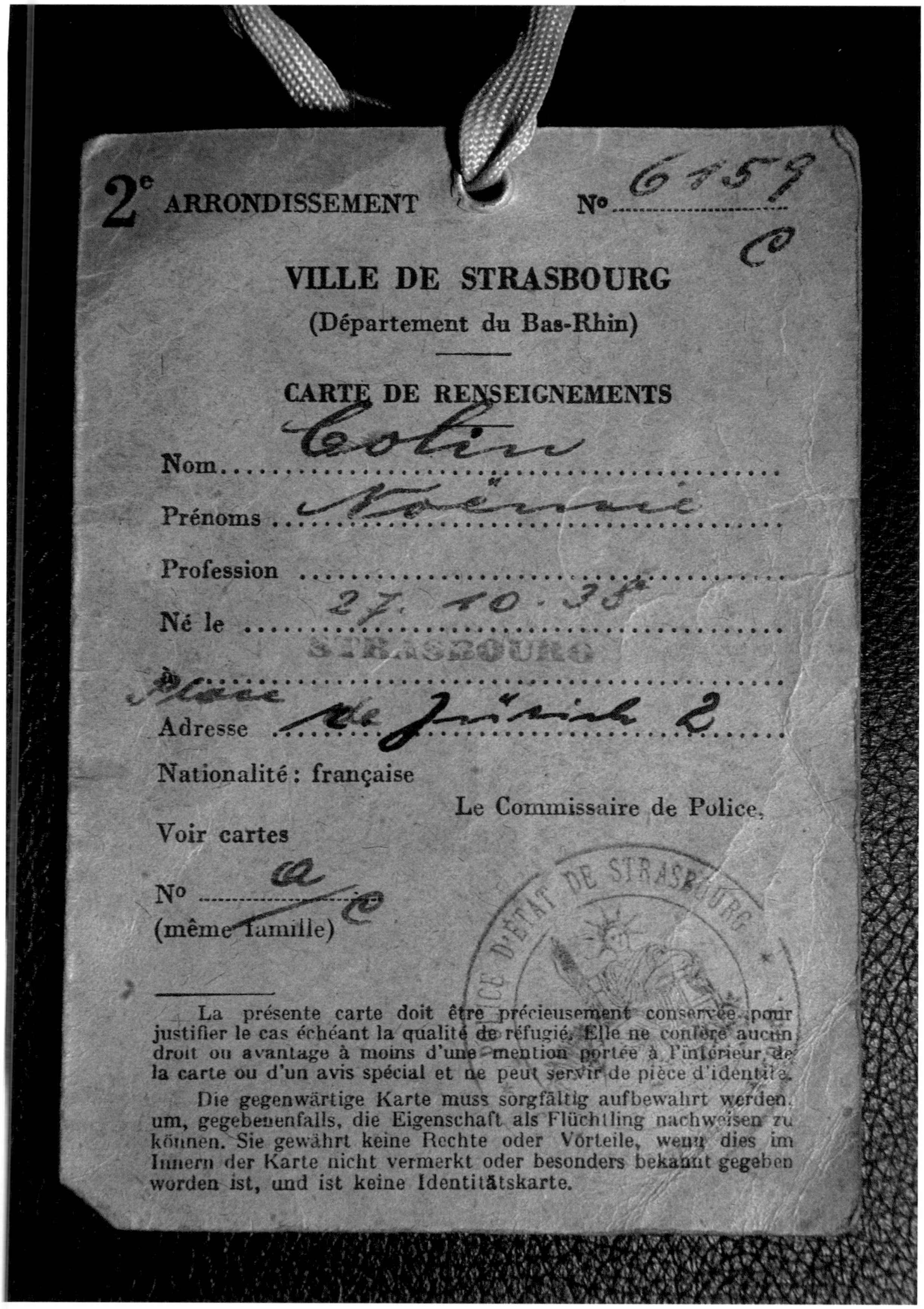

2e ARRONDISSEMENT   No *6759*

VILLE DE STRASBOURG

(Département du Bas-Rhin)

—

CARTE DE RENSEIGNEMENTS

Nom .... *Colin* ....

Prénoms .... *Noémie* ....

Profession ....

Né le .... *27. 10. 38* ....
STRASBOURG

à ....

Adresse .... *Place de Zürich 2* ....

Nationalité : française

Le Commissaire de Police,

Voir cartes

No .... *a/c* ....
(même famille)

———

    La présente carte doit être précieusement conservée pour justifier le cas échéant la qualité de réfugié. Elle ne confère aucun droit ou avantage à moins d'une mention portée à l'intérieur de la carte ou d'un avis spécial et ne peut servir de pièce d'identité.

    Die gegenwärtige Karte muss sorgfältig aufbewahrt werden, um, gegebenenfalls, die Eigenschaft als Flüchtling nachweisen zu können. Sie gewährt keine Rechte oder Vorteile, wenn dies im Innern der Karte nicht vermerkt oder besonders bekannt gegeben worden ist, und ist keine Identitätskarte.

Identity card of Naomi, which was hung by a shoelace around her neck throughout the war

David Cassuto – Italy

David was born in Florence (September 27, 1937) to Nathan and Hannah Cassuto, a Florentine family that had lived in the city since the middle of the sixteenth century. They had been among those expelled from Portugal who reached the city after about fifty years in Turkey. David was the second of four children: Shoshana, the eldest, followed by David, Daniel and Chava. Chava did not survive the war after she was forcibly separated from her mother.

David's first years passed pleasantly. He was a member of an educated, Orthodox family, aware of Florence's significance as the city of the Renaissance and their Jewish-Portuguese background. These two facts determined David's future character. David and his sister Shoshana would go out every Sunday with their father to tour the hills of Florence, and in that way they were introduced to its very special landscape. Their father, who was a well-known ophthalmologist in the city and chief rabbi of the Florence Jewish community, was also an experienced bicyclist. He would take Shoshana on the crossbar and David on the handlebars. At some point he would tie the bicycle to one of the trees, and they would continue on foot to see the Tuscany landscapes, picking wild strawberries, gathering olives, and bringing their booty back to their mother, who would make from them sweet jam and pickled olives.

These outings were excellent opportunities to tell the children Bible stories and tales from the history of Florence, such as the stories of Boccaccio, edited of course for anything unsuitable for five- and six-year-old children. Sometimes they made their outings around the artworks of the greats of the Renaissance in the museums and public buildings, where they learned about the great artists, together with Bible stories and Greek mythology, with their father preparing them for life in the shadow of these universal geniuses.

On Friday nights around the Sabbath table, their father would enrich them with everything to do with the Jewish people, the Land of Israel and the Torah of Israel. Their mother encouraged them to write letters to their grandfather and grandmother in the Land of Israel, letters that apparently were never sent.

Times became difficult. At the end of the summer of 1943 the Germans conquered northern and central Italy. Their father was very involved in saving his townspeople, and in saving the many refugees who arrived in Florence from the north and west of Europe. On November 29, their father was caught by the Gestapo, and a few days later their mother and their uncle Shaul Campaniano were caught while dangerously trying to free their father from prison (the Cassuto children learned of the many saved by their father, Nathan, only many years later).

The good times had ended. The three children were separated from their parents and hidden by Christian families who saved their lives. David had to get used to a foreign lifestyle and non-kosher food with the Colci family, who took him in. It was not easy for him. The grandmother emerged from her hiding place to convince him to eat everything he was offered. Every Sunday he had to go to church, and every night to go see some action movie. One day, in the foyer of the movie house, a German soldier approached him, attracted by the blond boy, and wanted to pick him up in his arms. The screams of the terrified David rose to the heavens. From that day on, they left him alone at home. The danger was too great.

While hidden under the blankets, scared of the dark and the loneliness, he would have nightmares and his mother would come to him in his dreams. It seems the fear of being abandoned had left scars. David would wake up in a cold sweat. He would cover himself again with the blanket, recall the outings with his father and his mother's caresses, trying not to fall asleep and dream, until the family came back from the movies.

Nathan and Hannah were taken to Auschwitz. Nathan was killed, but Hannah survived and joined her children in Palestine. The war ended. After the war their Aunt Hulda and their maternal grandparents Digioacino collected the children, and in accordance with the parents' last will and testament boarded the ship *Princess Catherine* and entered Palestine legally with the help of Yitzhak Ben-Zvi (the second president of Israel). Their grandfather, Moshe David Cassuto (who had been invited by Chaim Weizmann, the first president of Israel, to teach at the Hebrew University), and grandmother Simcha, who had already made aliyah in 1939, took the children into their care.

The children grew up for seven years in their grandparents' home, with their grandparents bringing them back to the lifestyle to which they had been accustomed before the "Flood," and to an almost normal childhood. And very slowly, the children regained their physical and mental health. The family were members of the small community of immigrants from Italy. They had a small synagogue. At the Spitzer School on Hanevi'im Street in Jerusalem, ex-Italians used to get together on the Sabbath and Jewish festivals, which is how David became experienced in the Italian liturgy. He read his first *haftarah* [portion from the Prophets] at the age of eight.

One day the family learned that their mother had survived the death camps. The children awaited her breathlessly. The encounter was not easy. David had dreamed of a soft, loving mother. However, it was a woman on whom the signs of suffering and the death camps were very visible who came back to them. After not too long she got back to herself. She started to work in Hadassah as a laboratory technician. On May 13, 1948, she was killed in the atrocious attack by the Qawuqji forces on the convoy to Mount Scopus, and she was recognized as a soldier who had fallen in the line of duty.

Pain yet again traumatized the children. The grandparents had a new task – to also heal this wound.

When David was approaching the age of thirteen – the age of Jewish adulthood – his grandfather prepared him to read from the Torah. A year later the grandfather died, and David continued to grow and develop under the watchful eye of Grandma Simcha, who now had to act as parent and educator for the children.

David completed his high school studies at the Ma'aleh School in Jerusalem. He was enlisted in the army and served in the Parachute Nachal Brigade. In 1956 he took part in the Sinai Campaign, at the forward post of the unit in which he served. As a member of the Nachal [which combined army with settling the land] he was inducted into Kibbutz Lavi, where he met the woman who would become his wife, Naomi née Cohen.

In 1958, after the army, he registered to study architecture at the Technion in Haifa, which he completed in 1963. In the Six-Day War he took part in the conquest of the West Bank. In 1973 he opened his own office. As part of his work as an architect, he designed and built public buildings, synagogues and many settlements, and the holy aspect in architecture became his professional specialty. In the 1970s he was appointed chairman of the Association of Italian Jews in Israel. Ever since, for about thirty years, David has served in a volunteer capacity in this very special position.

In 1993 David became a member of the city council of Jerusalem and afterwards deputy mayor, a position he filled in an active and dynamic manner. Cultural activities in the city tripled during his time in office. In 1998 David was elected a member of the board of Yad Vashem, the Holocaust memorial center. Among the prizes he won were, in 2005, the highest Italian title of nobility, Commendatore (the Italian president, Azeglio Ciampi, and prime minister, Silvio Berlusconi, signed the certificate). His expert knowledge about the history of Jerusalem, the Shoah of Italian Jewry and architecture still today act as a catalyst for his public work, studies and creative work.

His love for the Jewish people and for the Land of Israel, his homeland, and Italy, the land of his birth, have made David a bridge between these two formative cultures: between Italian humanism and the abstract thought of the Jewish people. The Center for Italian Jewry with its ancient synagogue, Judaica museum, Research Institute for Italian Jewry and the Preservation Center, all managed by David, have become models to be emulated. And indeed, in a country made up entirely of groups of different peoples and origins, this is an example of how to lay out and document our origins. Italian Jewry has thus become a trailblazer, and David is the one leading the work.

David and Naomi have six children and seventeen grandchildren.

David Cassuto, Jerusalem

Diary of circumcisions carried out in the period 1937–1943 by David's father, Rabbi Dr. Nathan Cassuto, who perished in the death march leaving Auschwitz

[pp. 116–117] The star that was attached to the clothes of Hannah Cassuto, David's mother, during the period of persecution in Italy

Naomi and David Cassuto in their home in Jerusalem

The Cassuto family, Jerusalem

121

Lisa Steinfeld – Slovakia

Elizabeth was born in 1928, the second daughter of Zalman and Miriam Schwartz, the younger sister of Valera, in Ailok, a small town near Bratslava. Her father managed the estate of Count Esterhazy in the village. When Elizabeth was four years old, her mother became very ill and was removed to a hospital. She never saw her again, and her fate is not known.

Zalman brought Clara Fischer into the home to raise his daughters, and she remained with them until her death. The girls considered her their mother. The family moved to Komarom when Elizabeth was in first grade, and they also lived in Nove Zamky. The sisters were active in Hashomer Hatzair in Komarom, where they took Hebrew names: Elizabeth became Tzippora and Valera became Tamar.

In 1938, on the day the Hungarians overran the region with the support of the Nazi government, Zalman Schwartz was arrested for allegedly spying on behalf of the Czech government. His close relationship with Count Esterhazy, who was a member of the Czech government, was given as proof. Zalman was a colorful character, and the family believes that a man who owed him money accused him of spying in order to default on his debt.

Zalman spent a year in prison, where he was tortured. He was finally released and stripped of his Czech citizenship. During this time the girls were left without an income, and Clara Fischer stayed with them and worked together with the girls at various jobs in order to survive. In 1939, upon Zalman's release from prison, the family was exiled to a camp for stateless people (mostly Jews) in Garange, near Budapest, Hungary. It was a terrible camp where the inmates had nothing to do and were under constant surveillance. After a few months at Garange the girls were moved to the Jewish orphanage in Budapest.

In 1944 Zalman was released from Garange, and he picked up his daughters from the orphanage and took them back to Nove Zamky. During their absence much of the Jewish population in the area was annihilated, including close family. That year the family worked for a while on a sugar plantation in the country and was interned in the ghetto of Nove Zamky. Zalman was drafted into the Jewish brigade of the Hungarian army and also was on lists for deportation. He escaped the various conscriptions and interments four times until he was captured and taken to a concentration camp.

Soon afterwards the girls and Clara were rounded up and sent to Auschwitz. During the four days they spent on the train to Auschwitz Clara's hair turned completely white, despite the fact that she was only thirty-four years old. She was sent immediately upon arrival to the crematoria.

After three months in Auschwitz the girls were transferred to Allendorf, a small town in Germany, where they worked as slave laborers in a munitions factory making bombs.

In 1945, after a long march and liberation by the Americans, they returned to Nove Zamky in the hope of finding members of their family who had survived. With other refugees, they lived in the synagogue, which had been turned into a temporary shelter for survivors by the Jewish community. When they discovered that their father had survived the camps but died of typhus on the way home, they decided to immigrate to Israel. Only two uncles survived the camps. They remained in Nove Zamky, with broken hearts and in bad health. One of them died soon afterwards and the other eventually remarried, had a son and died in 1987.

They joined a Hashomer Hatzair group that traveled to Italy to await the chance to enter Palestine. In 1947 Elizabeth married Alexander Shmuel Steinfeld, who had spent most of the time during the war disguised as an Aryan and working as a Hungarian laborer in Germany. Alex was a skilled mechanic. He came from Tissaeyluck on the border between Slovakia and Ukraine. He too lost most of his family, except for two sisters, who immigrated to the USA.

They had plans to immigrate to the United States as well but changed their minds in 1948 and came to Israel instead. Their son, Yigal George, was born in Italy shortly before they left for Israel.

The family lived in Acco for four years. During this time Alex opened a garage in Haifa. In 1951 their second child, a daughter, Nurit, was born. They built a house in Tzur Shalom soon afterwards. In 1958 the family moved to the United States and lived in New York for twelve years. Nurit and Elizabeth returned to Israel in 1970; Alex and Yigal joined them for a while but Alex died soon afterwards at the age of forty-nine. Yigal returned to the States where he lived and worked as a chemical engineer until his death in 2007. In 1980 Elizabeth married Dov Kolin, a Hungarian survivor, and lived with him for twenty years in Arad. Following his death and the deterioration of her health, Elizabeth moved to Jerusalem to be near her daughter.

Despite all the hardships and loss she has endured and her failing health, she continues to be a lively, creative person who loves an adventure, growing plants and art.

Nurit Steinfeld, her daughter

The Steinfeld family in Be'er Sheva

Yossi Weiss – Slovakia

I remember exactly my fourth birthday, my last memory of a normal childhood. We then lived in Slovakia – my mother, Charlotte, father, Ludovid, and I – in the town of Topolcany. Early in the morning I was dressed for a party and told it was my birthday. A few days earlier I had learned from my mother to recite the poem "When We Married the Mosquito." For the occasion we were honored with the presence of Mrs. Wertheimer, who lived above us. After my successful recitation, I was praised by my parents. Mrs. Wertheimer gave me a blue bag containing glass marbles. At the same time, she waved a bar of chocolate, which I would get in return for a kiss. Since my aesthetic sense was already well developed at the age of four, I agreed on one condition – that I would kiss her daughter. I do not remember if I kissed her, but I did receive the chocolate to the accompaniment of cries of wonder at my excellent taste, or perhaps just my chutzpah.

My mother taught at the Jewish school. My father was a farmer, mainly growing sugar beets. Since my mother was busy all day, I was brought up by a German governess who was called "Schwester" [sister] by everyone. She was dismissed by Mother even before I became four, because according to my mother, she hated me for being Jewish and used to serve me boiling food at meals.

About five months after my birthday, some five policemen, known as Guards, turned up at our house. They wore black uniforms with forage caps shaped like boats. They were locals, and some knew my father. Within a few moments my father was told to go down to the street with his family. There was of course no opportunity to resist, since they all carried rifles with bayonets. Apart from a little case whose contents I do not know, we did not take anything with us. In the street we were ordered to climb into a big truck. There were other families sitting in the truck, and it started to move off to the railway station.

There a lot of Jews were already waiting. After not much time we boarded a train. This was a normal passenger train, not a freight train, but the crowding was dreadful. The crying and shouts continued for the entire length of the journey. I don't remember how long we traveled, but in the end we arrived at a small town called Zelna. This was an enormous transit camp where they brought together Jews who had been expelled from their homes. We were welcomed by the sight of enormous huts into which we were herded. Only towards night did we receive a bit of bread and some hot tea. The sanitary conditions were awful and the cold was unbearable. The guards beat us and shouted at us.

Here it should be pointed out that the Slovaks were even worse antisemites than the Nazis, and they took pride in enforcing the race laws even more punctiliously than them.

In the morning it was decided who should be sent where. Complete families were loaded on trains and sent to the extermination camps in Poland. We had a stroke of luck and were sent to a labor camp called Novky. I recall that the conditions there were bearable. The men worked in small factories related to the war effort, which meant help to the German army, which had not yet entered Slovakia.

After a short time, without knowing to this day who it was who helped us leave, we managed to get out of the concentration camp. My father and his two brothers went back every morning to work in the camp, and my mother and I lived in the small town nearby. My father warned us always, irrespective of what happened, to stay there and wait for him, because he would come to collect us if something happened. In the meantime the Jews opened a defense front in Banska Bystrica (into which Haviva Reich was parachuted). My father and his brothers ran away to there from the labor camp, and when the Germans gained control of this front, all the Jews fled from the town.

My father, who was sure that we would in any case arrive with all the escapees, was murdered by the Germans; we were told this after the war by someone who had witnessed it. When we saw that father wasn't coming back, my mother and I understood that we had been left alone. Then commenced an endless journey through the snow-covered mountains. Sometimes we managed to find shelter for payment with Slovak farmers. But hunger and the cold were our constant companions.

In the spring of 1945, when the war ended, we returned to our town of Topolcany on a Russian tank. My mother went back to teaching, and after a short time, when I was eleven and already a member of Hashomer Hatzair, I decided with my mother's agreement to go to Palestine.

Since I was a minor, it was decided to attach me to a man called Funk; I received the name of his son who had perished in the Shoah – Michael Funk. My uncle, my mother's brother, who was living in Palestine in Shefaya, had agreed with my mother that when I disembarked from the ship, the *Campo Dolio*, in Haifa, he would come to collect me. However, when the boat anchored in Tel Aviv I disembarked full of enthusiasm and got on a Jewish Agency bus that took us to an immigrants' camp in Raanana. My uncle, who didn't know my name had been changed, waited in vain. I was completely lost. After a few days I remembered that my uncle must certainly be worried and decided to travel to him

in Shefaya. With a small rucksack I left the camp, a child of eleven. I knew three words in Hebrew, Zichron Yaakov and Shefaya. I stopped a jeep in which sat a driver and an older, bearded man. To my delight the bearded man spoke Russian, which was how we spoke the whole way. He told me he was Yitzhak Sadeh [the founder and commander of the Palmach, the pre-IDF military units, before the State of Israel was born].

On the way up to Zichron in the direction of Shefaya they dropped me off. I started to run in the direction of Shefaya. There I came to an abandoned quarry, where I almost fell into an abyss and lost my life. With bleeding hands I reached the house of my uncle, who didn't know whether to cry or to laugh when he saw me. I spent six years in Shefaya. Afterwards I was enlisted in the navy. When I was released from military service, I worked at various jobs but in the end I started to work in the merchant marine. I loved the work and within a short time I was appointed a bosun.

In 1964 I finally married Michal. I am father of four wonderful children and grandfather, to date, of seven grandchildren. I am the husband of a wonderful wife, happy with life and hope this will continue forever.

Yossi Weiss, Zichron Yaakov

Yossi Weiss and his grandson Assaf

Embroidered tapestry, made by Yossi's mother

The Weiss family at their daughter's home, Tzur Moshe

Rachel Agiv – Libya

My mother, Rachel Agiv, was born in Tripoli, Libya, in 1930, to my grandmother, Asi, and grandfather, Mordechai. There were three sons and two daughters in the family. When the Second World War broke out my mother was ten years old. Libya at that time was under Mussolini's rule.

Since my mother and the family members had British citizenship, and on account of the cooperation between Mussolini and Nazi Germany, the entire family were taken as prisoners of war and transferred to the Bergen-Belsen concentration camp.

The time there was awful. Her father and older brothers, Victor and Abraham, did forced labor. In the camp they suffered from hunger, cold and deprivation, and their lives hung by a thread, not knowing what each day would bring.

She remembers her little brother Gabriel crying constantly at that time, because of hunger, cold and fear. My mother remembers that period as hard and traumatic. All the dead and the dying around her marked her greatly. Even today it is hard for her to talk about that time and she hardly shares her experiences with us. This was the climactic period of the war, and the family witnessed the Allies' bombing raids on Germany, which only added to the sense of fear and helplessness. Mother has described the nonstop bombing every evening. All they could do was to raise their eyes in prayer until the danger had passed.

After about a year in Bergen-Belsen, the family was transferred to Italy to a place called Villa Artzo. They were kept there in a holding camp with other prisoners of war. There they received better conditions since they were prisoners of war, and received food parcels from Britain via the Red Cross.

My mother's father passed away young in Italy, at the age of forty. He apparently died of a broken heart from the traumas of imprisonment and the war, which he could not handle. He was buried in Italy, where he remains to this day. In recent years the family has tried to check out the possibility of bringing his remains to Israel, but the cemetery has been plowed over and no longer exists.

At the end of the war, after the Allied victory, the family returned to Libya following a journey through Europe. There my mother married my father, the late Gabriel Agiv. There too their oldest son, Shalom Agiv, was born.

In 1951 my parents made aliyah to Israel together with Shalom, who was just a few months old, and they lived in the Kfar Yona transit camp. From there they were transferred to the Sakia ma'abara [absorption camp], which today is Or Yehuda.

The family lived in this ma'abara in an area of tents, in a leaky tent. My mother remembers also this period as traumatic. In the winter the tent flew away in the wind or was flooded by the rain, and they were without electricity or water or the minimum to keep body and soul together. At that time epidemics of typhoid and malaria were common, and a new baby that was born to my parents died right after birth. My parents' attempts to get an entitlement to a hut, which in those days was the ultimate dream of a new immigrant, failed. My father, the sole breadwinner, worked at a variety of temporary jobs, and deprivation and poverty were their daily lot.

Afterwards, a district was built nearby for new immigrants from North Africa and Iraq, Ramat Pinkas, where my parents also went to live. The rest of the children were born there, and today the family consists of five sons and two daughters.

Our home was small, without many possessions, but was rich in spirit, values of love of the Land of Israel and of one's neighbors, and hospitality.

My late father worked as a construction worker and my mother as a cleaner to help provide a living for the family. In 1994 my father passed away suddenly from a heart attack. My late grandmother lived in a separate unit in the yard, where she was looked after until her dying day, mainly by Mother, who thereby fulfilled the biblical injunction "Thou shalt honor thy father and thy mother."

All the sons served in the army, and two were officers. Some went on to higher education.

Today, thank God, all are married, and are parents and grandparents.

My mother, who should be blessed with a long life, is religiously observant. That is the way she brought us up – with a great deal of patience, tolerance and respect for others. Both at times of economic stringency and in good times, my mother remained strong in her faith and ingrained in us the faith that "he who trusts in God will be surrounded by God's kindness."

Reuven Agiv, her son

The Agiv family in Ramat Pinkas

139

Ehud Walter – Romania

I was born in Haifa, Palestine, in September 1926 to Rachel and Baruch Walter, the younger brother of Sarah and Nili-Tova. Due to the economic difficulties of those times, my parents were obliged to leave the country for the Transylvania region of Romania in 1928. Our home there was a Zionist one and I was a member of a Zionist youth movement until I was sent to the camps. Between 1940 and 1943 my father made me study electricity in addition to my evening classes. Being an electrician saved my life.

In 1940 my fate, like that of all the Jews of Transylvania, changed when the northern part of the region was turned over to Hungary.

I heard on radio broadcasts from London and Moscow what was happening in the Second World War. I knew that Nazi Germany was retreating on all fronts. In 1943, even though it was forbidden, the members of the Zionist youth movement got together to discuss plans for after the war. There, for the first time, I heard from a Jewish refugee from Poland the name Treblinka. To tell the truth, I could not believe my ears.

On the first day of 1944 I returned home happily from a meeting of the Zionist youth, where it was revealed that the prohibition on membership in the movement had been lifted. I did not know then that the joy was premature and that this was their way to get the names and addresses of members of the Zionist movement.

In the morning of March 19 we heard the news that the Germans had entered Hungary. I was at home alone with my mother. My father was on a business trip from which he never returned. He vanished for many years as though he had never been.

The Gestapo and SS started to limit our movements and to steal our property. Life became ever more difficult by the day. On May 2 an order was received to be ready the next day to be moved to a concentration area outside the town. The next day the march took place to the Jewish concentration point and transfer to the ghetto, which was an unused brick factory. Life in the ghetto was not too difficult but did not last for long. After three weeks, on May 27, 1944, we were sent by train to Auschwitz, which is where I saw my mother for the last time. Later I heard rumors that she had been shot by a German on a death march.

The day I am writing this is exactly sixty years to the day from when I arrived at Auschwitz-Birkenau.

When I got to Auschwitz I didn't know where I was. I had also never heard of the name of the camp before. Yet after just one day I already knew the truth about that terrible place. I was fortunate that after a few days they moved me to the Buchenwald concentration camp, and the next day from there to a work camp next to Brabag Werke, a synthetic petroleum plant. The work was extremely hard. I managed to hold on for several months, but toward September I became a *Muselmann* [the term for walking skeletons] and was returned to Buchenwald. Through great luck I was saved from certain death. I had already been allocated to a group intended for the crematoria and waited in a temporary holding area. Two Jews from my hometown with whom I had traveled in the train to Auschwitz suddenly saw me and brought Mickey Hartmann, who sent a note to the commander, and I was miraculously taken out of the group.

It would appear I remained in Buchenwald until the end of September. Afterwards I was returned to the factory, and on December 1, 1944, I came again to Buchenwald with a group of *Muselmänner*. As I helped an elderly Dutchman get off the truck, I suddenly felt a sharp smack on my shoulder. The Commandant was standing next to me. We were scared to death of him. To my astonishment he said to me, "You're a good boy. What is your profession?"

"Electrician," I answered.

"You will work as an electrician in the nearby villages," he said. (Since all the men had been called up to the war, there were no professionals left in the villages).

That's how I was saved a second time, this time by a German, Mueller. After the war I tried to find him, since I knew I owed him my life, but I was told that because he refused an order from a more senior officer he was shot on the spot.

Around February 1945 I asked to return to Buchenwald on the pretext that my family was there. To my surprise my request was granted.

I just managed to hold on during the last days of the war, and on April 11, 1945, I was liberated by the US Army.

On July 15, 1945, as in a dream, I saw the lights of Haifa. I had returned home!

I took part in the War of Independence and in 1951 I married Leah and started a family, two sons, Yitzhak and Ofir, and six grandchildren: Assaf, Elad, Hila, Efrat, Dror and Kinneret. I felt that was my revenge against them. I raised three generations after me, because I have also had the good fortune to see both a great-grandson and a great-granddaughter, Aviv and Ma'ayan.

That is my life's story in brief, the story of Buchenwald prisoner number 58853.

Ehud Walter, Kiryat Bialik

Information about Ehud Walter is courtesy of the Artifacts Department of the Yad Vashem Holocaust Martyrs' and Heroes' Remembrance Authority.

The prisoner's clothing of Ehud Walter, donated to the Artifacts Department of the Yad Vashem Holocaust Martyrs' and Heroes' Remembrance Authority in 1982

The Walter family in Kiryat Bialik

Shushan Cohen – Tunis

I was born on July 12, 1925, in Djerba to Camona née Cohen and Massud Cohen. (In Djerba the surname of all the Jews was Cohen.) I had a difficult childhood. The family was large and my father didn't earn enough to support us. When I was a child my father went to Tunis in the hope of finding a livelihood there. He stayed there a short time and sent us money, but not enough. So we all went by sailboat to Tunisia. We reached Sfax and I recall that from there we took a cab to Tunis. I was already a youngster of twelve and I wasn't in school. I started to work at a bakery and my younger sisters went to work cleaning houses.

My friends all had means, and that's how I learned to read and write. I also started to speak French – until then we had only spoken Arabic at home.

In 1943 the Germans entered Tunis. The Germans asked from the Jewish community that all the men aged seventeen to fifty report for work to save the homeland. It never occurred to us to flee. They took us in cattle trains to the town of Mateur and from there we went on foot to the farm of an Arab – Sachsaf. At the farm they housed us among ruins and stables, from which they did not even remove the manure.

I remember that one night, at the height of a very tough winter, a German entered the stable, beat us with a whip and ordered us to get up and to pull out carts that were stuck in the mud. When we returned to the stable at daybreak, worn out and soaked through, to rest for the few hours before we went out to work, I heard my neighbor, Avram, crying. He said he lost his shoes in the mud and mire, and without shoes his fate was sealed. I promised I would find him a pair of shoes by the morning and he quieted down. In the morning I gave him my shoes. For a week I went barefoot to work. My feet were injured from the gravel and stones, but blood didn't even flow on account of the freezing cold. The Jewish community occasionally sent us food and things, which was how I got a new pair of shoes. Yet Avram never forgot my help and he remained my best friend to the end of his life.

Two days later, a German on a motorbike with a sidecar stopped us when we came back from work. The motorbike was stuck and he ordered us to get it out of the mud. When we had gotten it out he ordered us to return to our places. We refused because we knew we would be severely punished for being late. He agreed to take us back to his own camp until the morning. There, he put us, wet and dirty, in a pigsty, to spend the night there. I will never forget the humiliation I experienced then. The pigs trampled on us and rubbed against us, and we were obliged to wallow in the mud and their excrement. The dreadful smell stayed with me for a month. I couldn't get rid of it, because there were no showers in the camp. We slept and worked in the same clothes with which we had left our homes. We never bathed. We were covered in lice. Clumps of them formed everywhere, even

in the nose and eyelashes. The food we received was off, and came in cans that we used at night for our bodily functions.

We had to carry on our backs the Germans' ammunition in the fields and mountains, in the rain and mud.

One day they took us to the front at a place called Zaghwan. On our way back they put as at night into a tunnel. We froze from cold. When we woke in the morning, to our surprise we found that not a single German remained in the area.

It was complete chaos. Arabs appeared and sold us pancakes. One of the prisoners suggested the two of us should run away. I suggested we flee along the railway tracks since we didn't know the way. When we reached Mateur, the town was besieged by the Germans. We decided to sneak in at night. Suddenly they shelled the town and we went in. The town was completely deserted. We were told the Jews were at Ras-el-Eini, three kilometers [about two miles] away. When we reached the farm, derelict, filthy dirty and covered in lice, the Jews wouldn't let us enter lest we infect all of them. They stripped us of our clothes and burned them, scrubbed us down and shaved us, taking off even our eyebrows and eyelashes.

I returned home after a three-month absence. The family was convinced I was no longer among the living since they had not heard a word from me.

I went back to working in the bakery, and did not step out from the house for fear I would be taken a second time to a camp. Only when I heard the British approaching did I go out into the street and saw British tanks. The Germans fled like dogs.

I reached Palestine in 1945. Young Zionists from Tunis reached Algiers and from there by plane to Cairo. The Jews of Cairo hosted us very well for several days. From there we traveled by train to Haifa, where we arrived on the eve of Chanukah. On the way we saw orchards. We also saw a man buying bread. I remember that night. I remember feeling that here life was best.

We went for agricultural training at Kibbutz Bet Hashita, and in 1948 after a great deal of hardship we founded Kibbutz Regavim. On the Black Sabbath [Saturday, June 29, 1946, the British rounded up all the Jewish leaders and men they suspected of anti-British activities and jailed them], I was arrested by the British and taken to Atlit. I was severely beaten by them because I did not want to give my name. They took us from there to Rafiah for three months, where we worked out in the sun the whole day. There I also learned Hebrew.

On the kibbutz, which has recently undergone privatization, I did all sorts of jobs over the years.

I was married for about forty years, though we never had children. When my wife passed away, over twenty years ago, I remarried to Zehava and we had one son, Amit. He got married about six months ago.

Today I no longer work, and I have just signed up for a photography course.

Shushan Cohen, Regavim

The Cohen family on Kibbutz Regavim in front of a photograph of Shushan's extended family

Rachel-Shela Altaraz – Macedonia

I was born with the name Rashele Zion in the town of Stip, Macedonia, Yugoslavia. It was only during a roots trip I undertook with my family in May 2006 to Macedonia and Kosovo that I discovered for the first time my real date of birth, October 3, 1935.

I grew up in a well-to-do home, the youngest daughter of a warm, loving family. I had two grown-up, married sisters, Julia and Bella, and a brother, Moise, who was a student and lived away from home.

In 1941 Yugoslavia was conquered by the Germans and annexed to Bulgaria. We experienced "invasions" of our large, spacious home more than once by the Germans.

On March 11, 1943, in the early morning hours, German and Bulgarian troops visited the houses of all the Jews of Stip and other towns in Macedonia. The Jews were taken from their homes and marched in processions to the railway station, where they were packed into freight wagons and sent to a concentration camp, which was the Monopol cigarette factory in Skopje, the capital of Macedonia.

Together with my family and many others I was incarcerated on the women's floor, in an enormous, dark room filled with bunk beds, under terrible conditions of overcrowding. I only met with my brother in snatched meetings on the stairs of the building, on the way to the toilets out in the yard. The Jews, including my family, were sent from Monopol to the Treblinka extermination camp. All were wiped out.

Bella, my older sister, was married to an Italian who lived in Pristina, Kosovo. A day before the consignment to Treblinka, we heard she would be released immediately from the camp because she had Italian citizenship. Suddenly and without any preparation, I, a child of eight, was pushed by my mother into my sister's arms. That was a trauma that would stay with me my entire life. The two of us ran away from the camp in the direction of Pristina, where we found refuge in her mother-in-law's house.

Her mother-in-law hated us. My sister left every day to work and I stayed at home with the hostile mother-in-law, who threw me out every day from the house and instructed me to come back only at nightfall. I also got food from her in dribs and drabs, in rusty cans, on the floor as though I were a dog. After long months of suffering, my sister couldn't stand up to the emotional and physical pressure and killed herself by drinking poison. The sight of my dying sister has not lost its hold on me to this day.

After the funeral, in January 1944, I was expelled from her mother-in-law's house and had to wander again, this time alone. A Jewish girl called Sonia brought me to her house. There I became servant for everything. I almost stopped speaking. Sonia treated me like a piece of furniture.

On May 14, 1944, the Jews were expelled from Pristina to the Sajmiste camp and from there to Bergen-Belsen. For some reason, they missed Sonia's house. The two of us fled the town that had been emptied of Jews, and started our wanderings. We managed to hide in a Muslim village. I became Salima. I was terribly run down and suffering from malnutrition, and became badly sick with typhus. I was admitted to the hospital and was then returned to the village in a very poor state and apathetic. After someone gave away that we were Jewish, Sonia and I were imprisoned in the jail and afterwards were transferred to a labor camp. I worked the whole day at cleaning in the camp. I was a distended sack of bones from starvation, and my body was one mass of wounds and bruises.

When Allied planes were heard in the sky above the camp, the gates were opened and the Germans fled for their lives. The prisoners all fled, including Sonia. She didn't wait for me. I couldn't run. I sat on the ground and sobbed for hours.

Someone took pity on me and brought me to a Jewish family in Pristina. Because of my very serious condition no one wanted me, and I was moved from family to family. I was sent to a Jewish orphanage in Belgrade. There for the first time I received proper treatment, both medical and psychological, and I started to study.

In 1949 I made aliyah to Israel with Youth Aliyah to Kibbutz Ein Dor. However, in this period too I was extremely lonely, and had mental breakdowns.

I met my husband, who was also from Yugoslavia, at Kibbutz Ein Dor, where he was serving as a soldier. Our acquaintance was renewed years later when he gave me support during a difficult time. His family took me to its heart and we got married.

We raised a healthy family in Jerusalem: a daughter, Orit, two sons, Mickey and David, and ten grandchildren.

Shela Altaraz, Jerusalem

156

[pp. 158–159] The blanket that covered Shela's sister's daughter, who died in infancy. The mother perished.

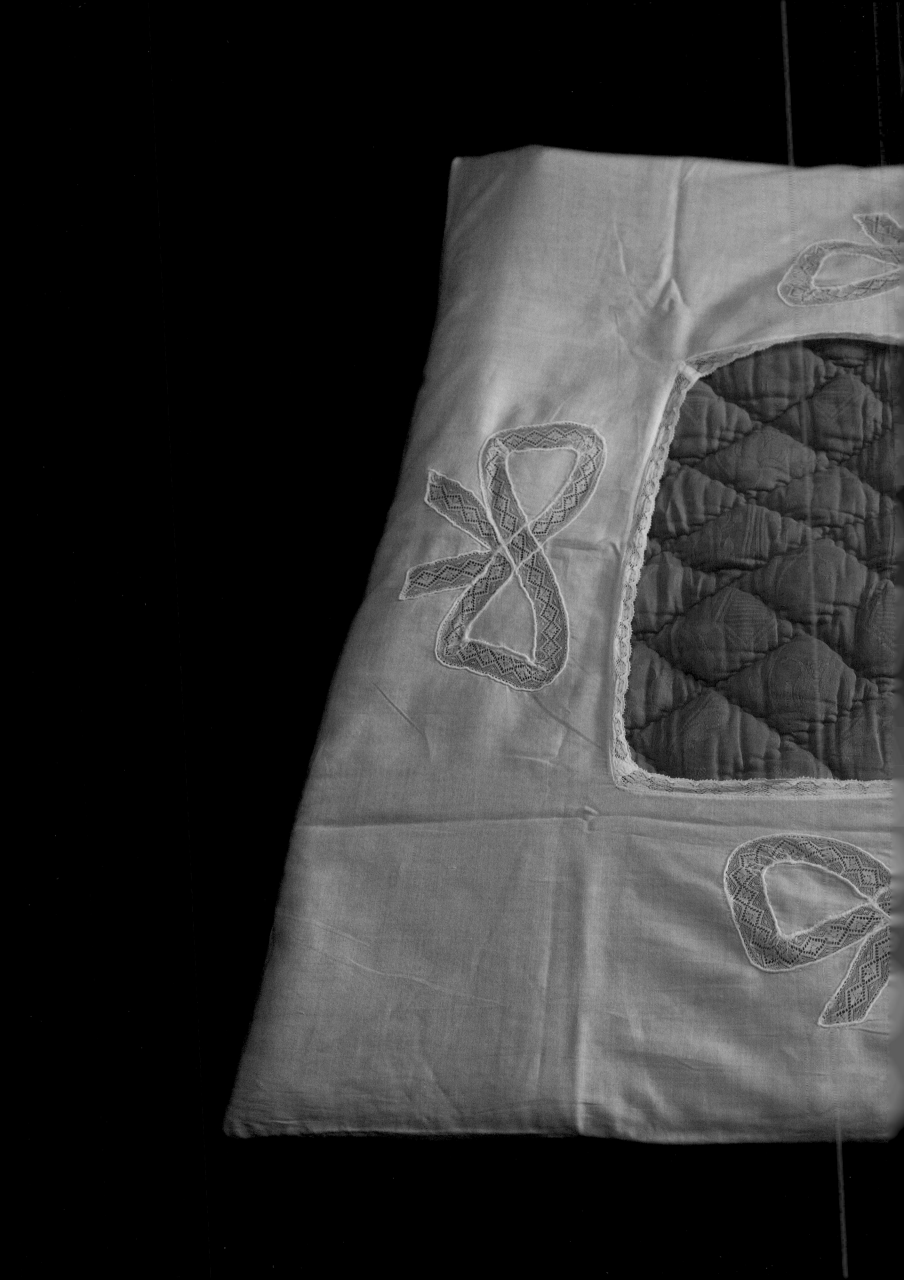

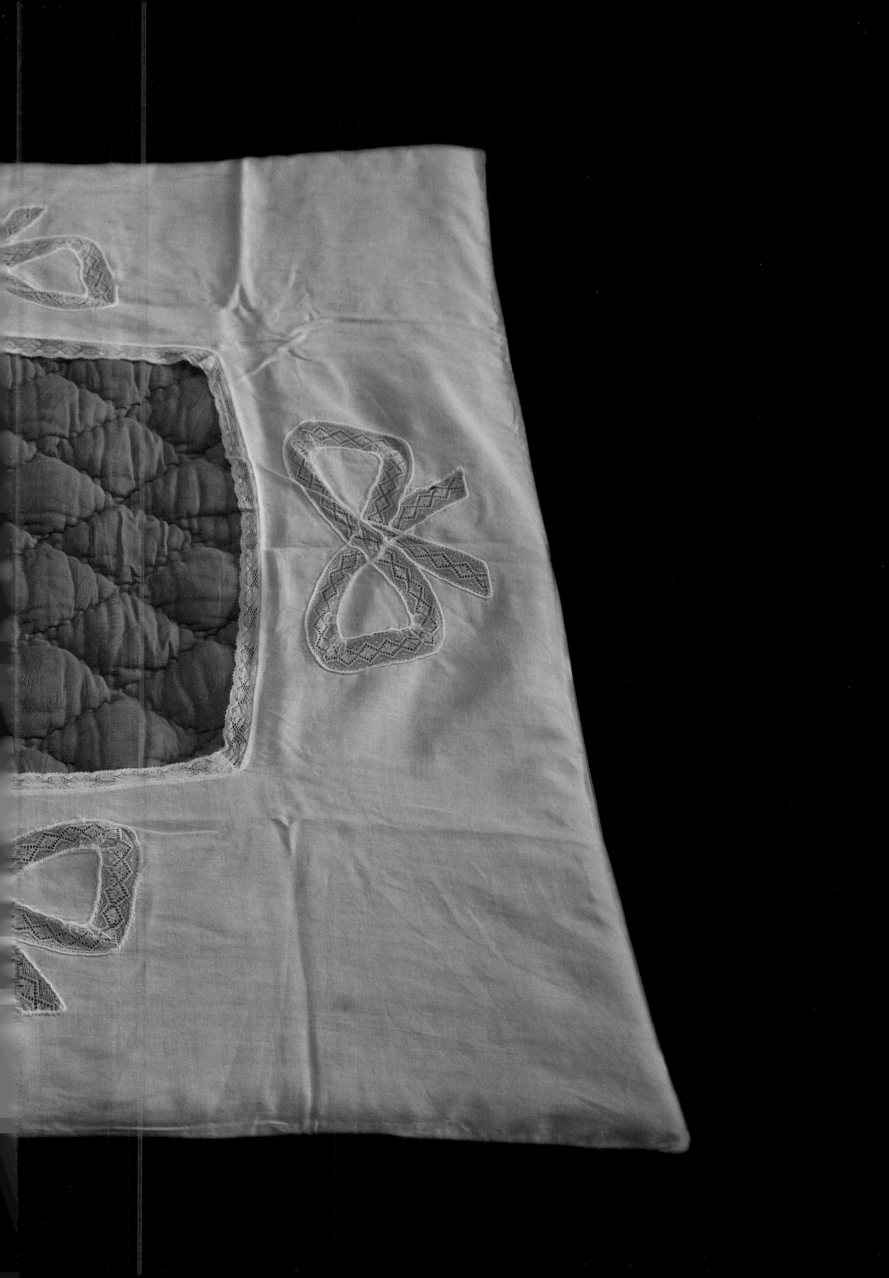

Avraham Altaraz —Yugoslavia

Born in Sarajevo, Yugoslavia, in 1931 to Mathilda and Moritz Altaraz.

He chooses to remain silent about the past.

He made aliyah in 1948.

From ship to truck and straight to the army.

He married Shela in 1951.

At the beginning in Israel he worked as a garage owner. After that and until his retirement he worked in the Prime Minister's Office.

He is the father of Orit, Mickey and David, and has ten grandchildren.

Avraham Altaraz, Jerusalem

Shela and Avraham Altaraz in their home in Jerusalem

The Altaraz family at their son's home, Jerusalem

Baruch Emmanuel – Germany

I was born as Bernard Baruch Emmanuel in 1929 in Hamburg, Germany, to Hannah-Martha née Goldschmidt and Mordechai Emmanuel. I was the fifth of eight children in a well-established, religious family. My father worked in a skins trading company and earned well. In 1933, when my father sensed the way the wind was blowing in Germany, the family moved to Utrecht in Holland, and from there to Rotterdam. All the children went to general schools and learned Jewish religious studies with private teachers. In the period when Holland was still not in the war, my parents helped organize visas and a place of refuge in our home for the hundreds of refugees who arrived from Germany.

My father drew up plans for our family to emigrate to Paraguay, where he had trading connections, but the German invasion beat us to it. On May 10, 1940, the German army invaded Holland and Belgium, and from there France. The illusion we had nurtured that Germany was interested in maintaining Dutch neutrality was shattered. Orders were issued by the Dutch government to arrest all German citizens, including the Jews. My father was also arrested.

At the beginning of 1940 when the mass arrests and the transports to unknown places in central Europe began, the Jews of Holland started to hide among non-Jewish citizens. This hiding was dubbed "diving" by the Jews of Holland, and those hiding were called "frogmen."

In the spring of 1943, when it was clear that the Germans were going to wipe out all the Jews of Holland, my parents decided to find a hiding place. For a family of eleven (my Aunt Mali had also joined us), this was no easy task. The family was divided up: my parents and Shalom moved into the house of Mr. Reiske, a Dutch acquaintance. My little sister Batya was adopted by a childless couple not far from Utrecht, and Aunt Mali with the six big children, myself among them, were taken up to the attic of a school, where Mr. Reiske worked as the caretaker. Mr. Reiske brought us food and we cooked in pots and pans we had brought from home. A short time later the entire family was arrested, but my father managed to get us freed using bribes. We returned to our previous home, which was completely empty of all that had been there, though at least we were all together again. It did not take long for two SS officers to turn up at our apartment with an expulsion order. To this day we do not know if Mr. Reiske had been involved in this. The fact was that all the Jews hidden by him were expelled to a camp. In the summer of 1943 the family was moved to the Westerbork transit camp near Amsterdam. The entire time we were in the camp we did everything we could to continue to keep the *mitzvot* [Jewish commandments], the Jewish festivals and Jewish studies.

On February 1, 1944, the family left with a shipment of 908 people to Bergen-Belsen. I worked at various forms of unnecessary hard labor, such as moving a pile of sand from one place to another and then back again. I also worked on the dreadful job of sorting and unpacking thousands of pairs of shoes that arrived from the death camps. One of the difficult things in the camp, apart from the hunger, was the endless roll-call parades, without moving, in snow and rain.

Toward the end of the war, within a couple of weeks, my father, my two smaller brothers and my eldest brother all died, from starvation and exhaustion.

At the end of April 1945, when the liberating armies were approaching, the Germans transferred the remaining Jews in the camp by train eastward, no one knew where. The objective was to hide the traces of the atrocities they had perpetrated. We traveled by train for thirteen days, without any sanitary arrangements and without food. Mother and my sister Bella were in one wagon, and Yona and I were in another one. My brother Shmuel stayed in the camp to look after my brother Shlomo, whose condition was critical. At one of the stops of the train I got out to look for food in the field. From a German farmer I got one fresh egg. I hurried to Mother, who was lying exhausted on the floor of the train, and gave her the egg. That was the last food she ate. The next day, on the Sabbath morning, my mother passed away, on Rosh Chodesh [the first day of the Jewish month of] Iyyar 1945.

The Russians liberated us. I was sick with tuberculosis and at the liberation weighed about fifty-seven pounds. I couldn't move.

Until 1950, when we moved to Israel, my brother Yona, my sister Bella and I were adopted by the Van Assen family, who looked after us with great devotion.

In my first year in Israel I studied in a yeshivah. Afterwards, my brother Shmuel and I joined Kibbutz Sha'alvim, which at that time had no water or electricity.

In 1958 I married my wife, Shifra, whom I had already known as a child in Holland. We had four children on the kibbutz. In 1966 we left the kibbutz for Jerusalem, where another daughter was born.

In Jerusalem I worked as a buyer for Shaare Zedek Hospital. Afterwards, I opened a store for grilled meat and poultry products.

Since I retired I have continued to get up at four in the morning, to start a Gemara *shiur* [lesson] at 4:45 a.m. I play tennis every day, go walking and enjoy my children and their families, three of whom live just nearby.

We have five children, twenty-seven grandchildren and one great-grandson.

Baruch Emmanuel, Jerusalem

The Emmanuel family on Kibbutz Sha'alvim

Ruti Ma'ayan – Romania

I was born in Czernowitz, Romania, in 1929 to Rivka and Mordechai Roll. Our family was a Zionist one. I had two uncles who studied law, and one was a Zionist leader in Romania before the outbreak of World War II. I was two and a half when my father died of heart disease. My mother, who was left alone, with the burden of earning a living on her, traveled to Vienna to study to be a seamstress for belts and bras. So I stayed with my Aunt Frieda, who looked after me until Mother returned from her studies. Then we moved in next to my grandfather and grandmother.

I recall that life was very difficult. My mother worked long hours to support us. The home was crowded, and I slept in the waiting room. The second room was my mother's work room. I did my homework in the kitchen. The nanny slept in the bathroom. I used to walk to school, which was called "Hebrew Language," where I learned Hebrew. I was a good student and a pretty girl. My main hobby was reading. When I was ten my mother remarried. My stepfather was a bookkeeper who had a son called Max.

Three days after my mother's wedding the Second World War broke out. At the beginning I didn't feel the war atmosphere. In 1941 the Russians overran Romania and I started going to a Russian school. When I was twelve, the Romanians decided to expel the Jews to German camps and we were transferred to the Czernowitz ghetto. In January 1942 we managed to leave the ghetto and to return home. My mother obtained a work permit and we thought we were protected from danger. However, in the end they came and took my family to the camp too. My aunt asked that I stay, but I didn't agree. I didn't want to be separated from my parents.

They moved us to a camp called Cariera de Piatra on the Dniester River. Fifteen people lived in a small hut the size of half a room. The toilets were outside. We froze from the cold. We were guarded by Ukrainians and Romanians. Every day they took people to so-called labor camps. They never came back.

I remember very well, one night they took us all of a sudden to the Tulchin ghetto. When they returned us the next day, we found the camp empty of old people and the mentally ill who had been with us there. They were murdered in cold blood and the Germans wanted to prevent our testimony of what had happened.

We were in the camp about a year, and in 1943 there were only about one hundred people left there. The Germans started to liquidate all the inhabitants of the camp. We managed to hide from the Germans in one of the huts with the help of Romanians whom we bribed, and so succeeded in staying alive. Afterwards we were moved to the Tulchin camp, where we stayed about a year.

In February 1944, before the end of the war, the Red Cross came to take orphaned children to an orphanage in Mogilev, Ukraine.

My parents managed to forge the identity card of a girl who had been killed so that I could leave the camp, which is how I became Sylvia Auslander. My cousin succeeded in getting me out of the orphanage and sent me back to Czernowitz, where a few members of my family still lived. That was May 1, 1944. Only three months later did my parents manage to return home.

My stepfather also spent time in jail. After the liberation, we moved in 1946 to Palestine.

I came with the illegal aliyah on the ship *Max Nordau*. It was really small, like a nutshell, and yet managed to carry 660 immigrants. When we reached Palestine the British captured it and transferred us to the camp at Atlit, and we were there two to three months. From there I moved to the absorption center in Hadera.

In 1950 I was called up to the army. I served in the Armored Division and completed the officers' training course.

In 1953 I married Gidon Mendel, who had been born in Berlin. We had three children, Tamar, Amnon Mordechai and Yoav Benzion. They have given us seven grandchildren, Lotem, Mor, Or, Nir, Nofar, Rotem and Alon Gidi.

During my life I have worked in a range of temporary jobs, including looking after children. Since my husband was against me going out to work, I didn't persevere in that.

My husband passed away in 1996. I had a stroke in 2007 and am trying to recover.

Ruti Ma'ayan, Kiryat Tivon

174

The lemon thrown at the train taking Ruti to the camp (see preface, p. 12)

The Ma'ayan family in Kiryat Tivon

Miriam Eiges – Poland

I was born in Lvov, Poland (today Ukraine), on January 26, 1937, with the name Marisha Gefaell, to Sonia and Bronislaw Gefaell. My mother was a bookkeeper and worked at the Blumenfeld paint factory. When the Germans entered Lvov I was four years and eight months old. I saw my father for the last time a short while after the Germans arrived in 1941. In all probability, my father perished in the Shoah. I have no information on when or where.

A few months after the entry of the Germans into Lvov, I moved with my mother to live in my grandmother's house, which was in the ghetto. At a later stage, when the Germans started constricting the ghetto, we had to leave my grandmother's house. Together with my mother's sisters and their families we moved to the Blumenfeld factory, which had been expropriated by the Germans and was included in the new ghetto area.

My mother hid me under her desk, while the rest of the family hid in the attic. Since my mother had a work permit and a senior position she was able to work for her living, and as far as she could, looked after the needs of the family in hiding.

In the autumn of 1942, when I was five and a half, my mother smuggled me out of the ghetto, and I never saw her again. As far as I know, my mother was killed in Lvov when the ghetto was liquidated in the middle of May 1943.

When I parted from her, and after passing through many other hands, I was handed over to nuns in the town of Ustrzyki Dolne, in the Carpathian Mountains close to the present border of Ukraine. There they changed my name to Maria Gerda. When the nunnery was bombed, the nuns and the children in their care were moved to a wooden hut in the forest. The children lived in one room and the nuns in the other. I stayed in the nunnery until June 1946. When I was taken from the nuns (by a friend of my aunt in Palestine), I stayed a short time in Lvov, and from there came to the town of Wroclaw in July 1946.

There I stayed a short while with the friend of my aunt, and the rest of the time at the orphanage. My mother had written from the ghetto to her sister Lonia in Haifa that she wanted me to go to her and to grow up with her. After many efforts and widespread searches while I was still in Poland, I was located by my aunt on November 18, 1946. I was adopted by my uncle, Shmuel Ben-Dov, and my aunt, my mother's sister, Lonia-Leah Ben-Dov.

My aunt Lonia had come to Palestine in 1935, and so was the only one left alive of my mother's ten sisters.

I reached Israel (then still Palestine) to the home of my uncle and aunt on July 28, 1947. There I had a warm home, with love and support, for me and two sisters younger than me, Irit and Ruti.

In this way, in 1947, at the age of ten and a half my wanderings ceased.

I did all my studies at the Leo Baeck school in Haifa. I was called up to the Nachal [combined army and pioneeing service] in November 1955. I married Gideon Eiges in August 1958. Between 1959 and 1962 I studied mathematics, physics and for a teaching diploma at the Hebrew University of Jerusalem. In the years 1962–2007 I worked teaching math at a high school in Jerusalem.

We had four children, Tamar, Itai, Nurit and Gil.

And we have been blessed with ten grandchildren: Rori, Omer, Gal, Neta, Amir, Michal, Naama, Shachar, Amit, Yuval, Noam and Ben.

Miriam Eiges, Modi'in

Embroidery by Miriam's mother, the only remaining memento of her

The Eiges family in Modi'in

Tony Weber – Belgium

I was born in Antwerp in 1927, to Mela-Leah Gottgold and Shlomo Siskind. My brother David is a year and a half older than me. My father's first wife bore him nine children. Five of them were killed. My father passed away when I was seven.

One Shabbat, when I was about four, I went with my father to the synagogue. I was not allowed to be among the men, so my father hid me inside his tallit [prayer shawl]. I played with the tzitzit [ritual fringes] and felt so safe in his arms.... That's one of my most beautiful memories.

We were Chassidim of Bobov, which has wonderful songs and tunes. At home we spoke Yiddish, but between ourselves my brother and I spoke Flemish. I attended a non-Jewish public school, where we studied the entire day. Only on Sundays and Wednesdays we learned part of the day, and then in the afternoon we studied Torah, Jewish laws, prayer and *Ethics of the Fathers*. My ambition since childhood to make aliyah started when I joined Bnei Akiva when I was eleven.

On May 10 the Germans invaded France, Belgium and Holland. Whoever could flee fled. Even the non-Jews. We too fled with the enormous crowd in the direction of the port. They told us that there were lots of British ships there that could take Jewish refugees to England. My mother was worried we would get lost, so she cut up kitchen towels into strips and tied us by our hands to each other. We were tied together for three days. I can still feel that horrible feeling till today.

One of my terrible memories is from the summer of 1942. We lived in an area populated mainly by Jews. One evening we heard trucks stopping under our windows and the stomping of German boots on the cobblestones. We hid behind the curtain and saw how they dragged out our neighbors in pajamas, beating them savagely with their rifle butts and whips. When the trucks were filled they drove off. They stuck to the door of each apartment a note on which was written, "Forbidden to open. The residents have left for an unknown destination." In the morning I ran round the entire area where we lived. Not a living soul was left.

My mother understood we had to run away. She sold everything that was left and bought my brother and me forged identity cards. She found someone who would smuggle us into Switzerland. The cleaning woman of the building agreed to hide her without us, because we might make a noise and reveal the hiding place. When we left the house for the last time, I instinctively took a silver spoon, which to this day I have kept with me. Our mother could have put us into a monastery, but she said, "I will never agree to hand over my children either to the Nazis or to a monastery. God will help me some other way. I will not give my children to Molech [pagan worship of infanticide]." My mother was caught when one day she went from the cleaner's house where she was hiding to bring food to an elderly man who was all alone and lived in our previous home. She was sent with the tenth transport to Auschwitz.

At the end of the summer of 1942 I traveled with a group of about ten people by train to the French border and from there went on foot into Switzerland. I was fifteen years old, the youngest member of the group. I had never before slept away from home. Since my father's death I had slept with my mother in the double bed. We were caught by Swiss soldiers, and after being held for five days, they pushed us with their rifles back over the border. In total the Swiss expelled thirty thousand refugees during the war, of whom only one hundred survived. My brother and I, using a Michelin map our mother had given us, managed to infiltrate back into Switzerland. We would walk at night and hide during the days.

There were a few points of light during that dark period, such as Maurice, the young man who carried me on his shoulders when I couldn't walk because of my injured legs, and who freed my brother from jail and attached us to a group he was leading that managed to cross the border. Or the couple that realized we were refugees and gave us all the food they had and directions how to reach a Jewish family in Nyon; with their help we managed to reach the Jewish center in Zurich, where they rented us rooms.

I became ill with tuberculosis and was sent to the hospital. I was placed in isolation. In the hospital I met Sister Annie, a Quaker, who was the first to wipe my forehead. She was my savior and looked after me until the end of the war.

I reached Atlit in Palestine via Barcelona in 1945 with the first boat that sailed from there. I first went to Kfar Chasidim and from there to Kibbutz Yavne, following my husband Aharon, whom I married in 1949. We were eleven years on the kibbutz. Afterwards we left for Tel Aviv. Over the years I studied interior design at evening classes at the Technion, as well as art at the university. I worked my whole life in interior design.

We have two children, Shira and Ro'i, and five grandchildren, Shachar, Eyal, Inbal, Daniel and Jonathan.

In 1952, during my first trip out of Israel, I visited Sister Annie. I continued to visit her almost every year. After she passed away, I still visit the Quaker community during every trip I make to Switzerland.

Tony Weber, Ramat Aviv

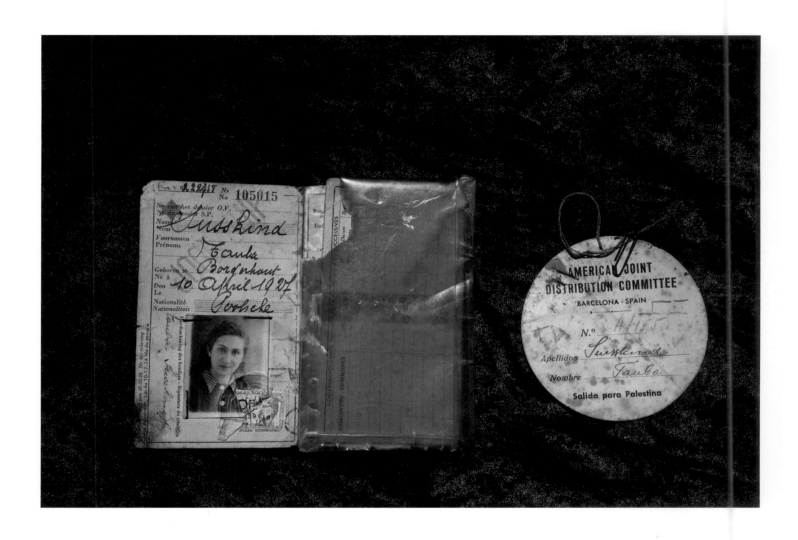

188   On the right: Certificate issued to people who had been stripped of citizenship, provided to Tony before she made aliyah

On the left: Identity card issued during the period of occupation, stamped "Jew," with a Star of David

▲ teaspoon, the last memento from her home, taken by Tony when she was already in the doorway on the day she escaped

189

190   Pajama trousers made by Tony's mother, which Tony used throughout the war. The patch was sewn on at the kibbutz.

Postcards written by Tony's mother from her hiding place in Antwerp to the hiding place of the children in Switzerland. The untidy handwriting indicated she was already without glasses.

Aharon Weber– Austria

I was born in 1921 in Baden bei Wien, a tourist town, to my mother, Carola, and father, Ignitz. I was the oldest of four brothers. My father had served in the emperor's army and after that worked in the Jewish community, and he passed away when I was bar mitzvah age. I went to a regular school and we went to Sunday school religion lessons. Afterwards I transferred to a commercial school at age fourteen.

And then Hitler came.

I remember that once they rounded up all the men of the Jewish community to clean the road with toothbrushes. On another occasion they took all the young people of the community to smash the synagogue furniture. Everyone was destroying things apart from me. I managed not to take part because the commander of the Nazis had studied with me in school. Later on they changed the commanders so that they should not have problems giving orders to Jews with whom they had studied together.

My mother was very religious. When there stopped being services at the synagogue, she sent me to a minyan [prayer quorum] in a far-off synagogue. My mother saw things coming. She understood it was no longer possible to stay in Austria, and she sent my brother and me to Palestine with Aliyah Bet in 1938. However, she did not understand or believe that they would slaughter them like chickens. Apparently she thought they wouldn't harm the elderly, especially if her husband had served in the emperor's army. She was deluding herself. She invested all the money she had in her sons so that they would survive.

She and my two sisters were murdered in Theresienstadt.

Beitar organized the transport of Aliyah Bet on a cargo ship. I boarded the ship on September 5, two days before Kristallnacht. After much hardship I reached Kfar Vitkin, and eventually Kvutzat Yavne. Since I was already seventeen and a half, I wasn't allowed to study like the rest of the young people on Youth Aliyah. I was assigned to work in the orchard, and I came down with malaria.

My brother, who arrived a bit later with the ship *Patria*, which sank, was younger than me so he could join in Youth Aliyah and managed to study. He died here at a young age due to misdiagnosis by a doctor. I never sat on a school bench again.

I enrolled in the Jewish Brigade in 1941. I returned to the kibbutz in 1946 and I married in 1949. Tony and I had two children.

I fought in the War of Independence, and I fought in all Israel's other wars as a reservist. I traveled every day under fire as the driver of the kibbutz truck to bring food to the people in Tel Aviv. Once I brought food in the truck to Jerusalem and the truck was damaged by fire from the Arabs. It is still there, to this very day, on the road to Jerusalem.

We left the kibbutz at the time of the Sinai Campaign, first to Bnei Brak, and a year later to Ramat Aviv.

Until 1967 I was a truck driver, and afterwards I went to work in diamonds, which is what I still do today.

Aharon Weber, Ramat Aviv

194

Tony and Aharon Weber in their home in Ramat Aviv

The Weber family in their home in Ramat Aviv

Shulamit Catane – France

בס״ד

I was born on Yom Kippur 5682 (1922) in the town of Homburg, Germany. I was the eldest in a family of five children. The family was bourgeois, very Orthodox and Zionist. We grew up in an enormous home of twenty rooms, with a large garden that bordered a wood. My father inherited the house from my grandfather. Father was a businessman. Mother was a housewife. When inflation rose, the metal factory where my father worked closed and antisemitism started to raise its head, my parents decided to leave for Paris.

In 1929 we moved to France. There I studied in public elementary and high schools. We had a private teacher for Jewish religious studies (Torah, prayer, Jewish history and Jewish laws), and a private teacher for general subjects on Sundays. Since we did not go to school on Shabbat, on Sundays we had to make up the material learned then. We celebrated Shabbat at home, in the synagogue, at family meals, by studying Torah and playing group games – ping-pong and chess with Father and Mother.

When the Second World War broke out in 1939, our childhood ended. In the summer of 1939 we went on vacation to Megève. My father, who had stayed in Paris, was arrested by the French as a foreign subject. After the conquest of France by the Germans, he was arrested by them as a Jew and sent on a death train to Auschwitz, where he was murdered. We learned of his death and the death of the rest of the Jews of Europe in the extermination camps only two years after the end of the war, when we sat *shivah* [the Jewish week of mourning] for him, as required by Jewish law.

Most of the difficult years of the war we passed in Megève. Most of the time without Father. Later on we moved to Rouen, where there was a small Jewish community. Mother bravely handled the role of head of the family. We all studied both general topics and Jewish religious subjects. At home we helped carry the water from the public pump and carry coal to the boiler for heating and cooking.

My wedding in the winter of 1942, during the war, to a childhood friend was done to make the release of my father easier, because my fiancé was French, the son of a family who were friends of my parents. However, the laws changed again, and Father was rearrested and sent, as I have mentioned, to Auschwitz.

At the end of 1942 our oldest son, Rafael, was born. He saw his father, my husband, very little, because he would travel as a Frenchman, without arousing the suspicions of the farmers, among the villages, bringing to his Jewish acquaintances tefillin [phylacteries] and tallitot [ritual prayer shawls], and also acted as a postman.

We managed to escape to Switzerland, a neutral country. One of the fishermen agreed, in return for all our possessions (our two blankets and the food vouchers for the three of us), to take us across Lake Geneva in a small boat at night. We didn't know if he would keep his promise or hand us over to the police, but we had no better alternative. We reached Geneva, where we stayed until the end of the war.

After the liberation of France we returned there, where my husband completed his studies as a librarian, archivist and historian.

After the State of Israel was established, we made aliyah in 1950 to Israel with five children, a tent and a few boxes, and went to Jerusalem. My husband was appointed principal of the French Alliance school. We rented an apartment near the then border (today Ramat Eshkol), and started a happy life in the beloved new state. That was the period of extreme austerity: without National Insurance, with breakdowns in the supply of water and electricity, cooking on a primus stove or kerosene burner, and no diapers. Yet our house was always filled with joy and friends. We had another five children. In the years 1962–1964 we went as educational representatives to France, and returned with two more babies. I completed my BA and a course in librarianship.

In the years 1970–1985 I worked in the Knesset [parliament] archives and afterwards as a volunteer at Shaare Zedek Hospital, and at the Yad Sarah and Emuna organizations. I received the Yakir Yerushalayim (Distinguished Citizen of Jerusalem) award in 2002.

I have been a widow for twelve years and live in an assisted living facility. Here too I am active and happy. I have eighty-one grandchildren and 205 great-grandchildren. My eleven children (one daughter died when she was a baby) and forty-five married grandchildren all have happy families. I arrange very large family get-togethers twice a year, apart from the various happy family occasions (weddings, circumcisions and bar mitzvahs).

My greatest joy is that all my descendants live according to the Torah, love each other and have excellent relations with me.

Shulamit Catane, Jerusalem

Shulamit Catane with her 140th great-grandchild, Hallel

The Catane family in Jerusalem

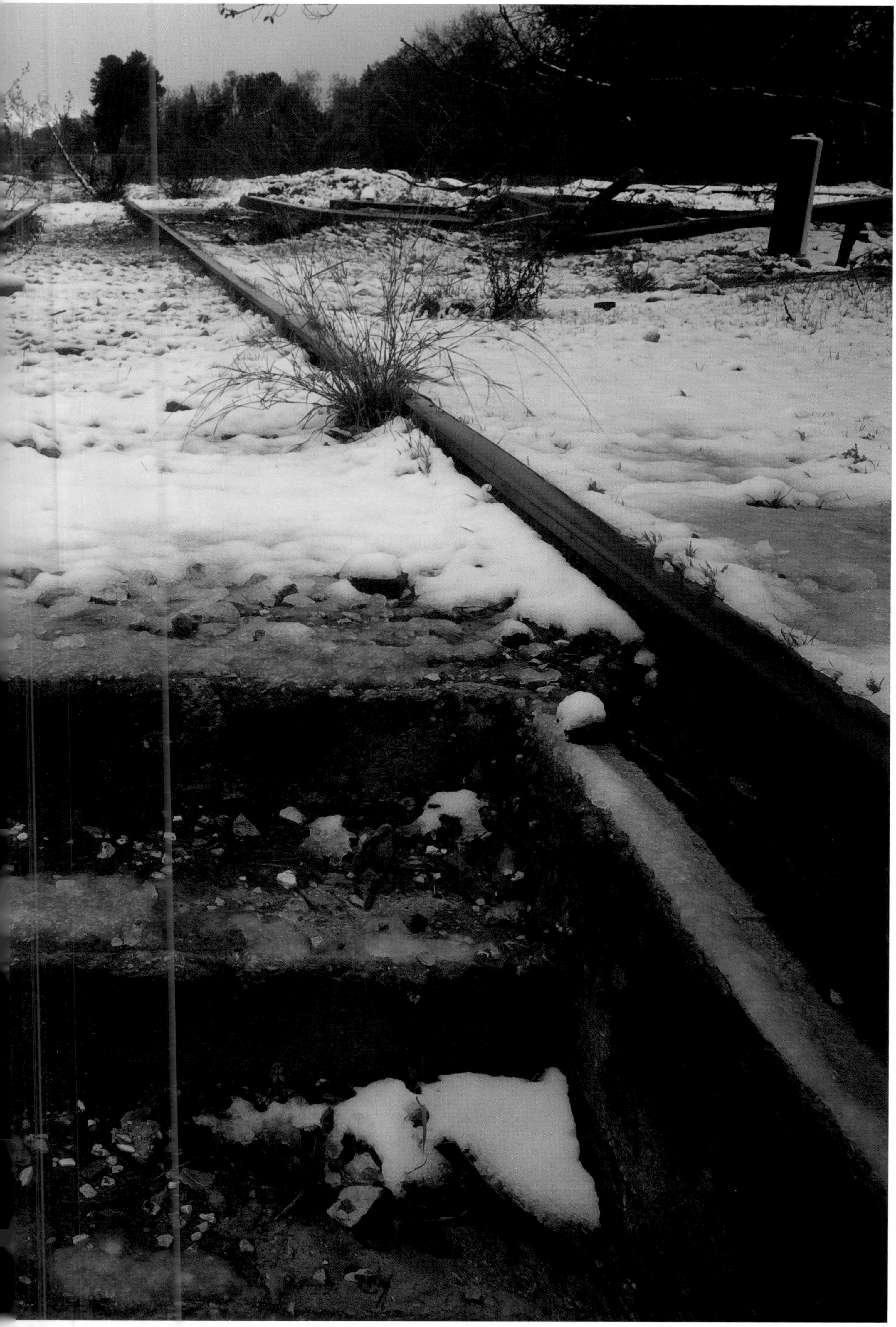